Catch YOUR Breath

GOD'S INVITATION TO SABBATH REST

DON POSTEMA

FAITH ALIVE®
Christian Resources

Grand Rapids, Michigan

Unless otherwise noted, the Scripture quotations in this publication are from the NEW REVISED STANDARD VERSION BIBLE, © 1989 by the Division of Christian Education of the National Council of Churches of Christ in the United States of America. Published by Thomas Nelson, Inc., Nashville, Tennessee 37213. Used by permission of the National Council of Churches of Christ in the United States of America.

Scripture quotations from THE MESSAGE © 1993, 1994, 1995. Used by permission of NavPress Publishing Group, Colorado Springs, CO.

Scripture quotations from *The Jerusalem Bible* © 1968, Doubleday, Garden City, NY.

We welcome your comments. Call us at 1-800-333-8300 or e-mail us at editors@faithaliveresources.org.

Library of Congress Cataloging-in-Publications Data

Postema, Don, 1934-
    Catch your breath: God's invitation to Sabbath rest /
Don Postema.
        p. cm.
    Includes bibliographical references.
    ISBN 1-56212-239-8
    1. Sabbath. 2. Sunday. 3. Ten commandments—Sabbath.
    I. Title.
BV111.P66 1997
263'.3—dc21

                                                    96-39925
                                                    CIP

10 9 8 7 6 5 4 3

Contents

Preface

This small study you have in your hand is a simple invitation to think about sabbath—and to *practice* it. Sabbath is certainly fascinating to study and think about. Yet, you can't get the full benefit of sabbath by only thinking about it as an interesting concept or a good idea.

I realized this most profoundly when I began writing these reflections on the sabbath. When I was asked to write this book, I was delighted. I have been reading, thinking, and even speaking about the sabbath for some time. I have listened to my Jewish friends relish their sabbath time. I talked with my mother and many others about Christian sabbath practices in the past and present. Our congregation spent six months in worship and study focused on sabbath and in developing personal and communal sabbath habits. I found all this enticing.

The writing, however, made me realize that my own sabbath practice was well behind my thinking. Perhaps that is why it was rather difficult to write. For I was continually challenged to *live* sabbath. The benefit of sabbath is not simply in the study of it but most assuredly in the practice of it—in *living* sabbath. Reading and thinking about sabbath is like reading travel brochures and dreaming about great vacation spots but never going there for a vacation. It is interesting. You can even learn a lot. But you can't have the experience unless you make the journey.

This book is something like a travel guide to an intriguing vacation spot. But I hope you don't simply read it quickly and put it down thinking, "I might like to go there some time." Rather, I hope that together we can experience a vacation with God—weekly, maybe even daily or minute-ly, as we respond to God's gentle invitation to sabbath rest.

I pray that your sabbath experience will deepen your friendship with God, with others, and with yourself.

Don Postema

Introduction

These reflections on sabbath have been written for Christians who wish to grow spiritually. The format encourages use with small groups. Of course, the book also can be used for private study, reflection, and spiritual growth. The group activities, quotations, and questions in the margins can be adapted to guide your personal reflections.

There are advantages in meeting, meditating, studying, discussing, and praying with a small group of two to twelve other people. Such a group provides us with a supporting community and gives us the opportunity to develop deep and meaningful relationships with people who are also on a spiritual journey. Being in a group keeps us accountable and honest and can help prevent us from deceiving ourselves as we develop new spiritual practices. I believe we need all the help we can get! A small group can provide prayerful encouragement as we learn from each other's setbacks and advances.

USING THIS BOOK

Every member—or couple—in your group should have a copy of this book. I suggest you hand it out either before the course begins or at the first session. You may want to ask group members to read the prologue before your first meeting so discussion can begin immediately, or read it (either aloud or silently) during your first session.

The prologue, Getting Acquainted, is an introductory chapter that lets group members get acquainted with the subject matter of the book. It also allows them to share their expectations for their future experiences with it. This will enable them to become acquainted as people on a spiritual journey into sabbath time and space. Even if people know each other already, sharing their expectations can move them to a deeper level of friendship.

You will notice that the other six chapters are divided into two columns. How these are read may vary from group to group and from session to session. Group members may read them at home, or you may find various ways to read them during the group session. I urge you to read the materials slowly, thoughtfully, and meditatively. I wrote these words not only for your head but also for your heart.

The writings in the smaller, right-hand column are meant to aid this slow, thoughtful reading. There you will find suggestions for personal and/or group reflection, invitations to meditation, provocative quotes for consideration, and suggestions for discussion. You may wish to add quotes, ideas, or questions of your own.

In these margins you'll find frequent quotes from *The Sabbath*, a contemporary classic on the meaning of sabbath for today. The author, Abraham Joshua Heschel, is a Jewish philosopher, theologian, and widely respected religious leader. Our thinking about the meaning of sabbath for Christians will be enriched by this extraordinary writer from a tradition in which the sabbath is so central. It has been said that it was not so much that the Jews kept the sabbath, but that, throughout their long, often painful, yet extraordinary history, the sabbath kept the Jews.

You will need at least an hour for each session; an hour and a half would be even better. Your session ought to be relaxed, not rushed, with adequate time to think, reflect, and talk. It takes time to contemplate spiritual questions, to listen to our own experiences and thoughts, to absorb new insights, and to make decisions about future directions in our spiritual life.

It is helpful to have a group leader to lead the meditations, direct the readings, and pace the discussions. The leader will certainly want to be a facilitator rather than a lecturer or outside observer—a servant of the group and a full and equal participant on this spiritual journey.

SETTING

It's important to establish an atmosphere that reflects your group's personality. Unless there are too many of you, sitting in a circle or semi-circle enhances group interaction. I like to have a table in the middle with a lighted candle or two, a cross, some flowers, or perhaps a Bible—some arrangement that establishes an appropriate setting for your time together. Lighting the candles before most people arrive or to mark the beginning of your meeting can help focus the group's attention. If group members don't know each other, provide name tags with first names written large enough to be easily seen by the others in the group.

I usually ask group members to enter the room in silence and to sit quietly until the meeting begins. Quiet music during this time helps people make the transition into the group setting and into the presence of God. Perhaps someone could play piano, guitar, or some other instrument. Or you could play some recorded music appropriate to the topic of the evening. Silence and/or music gives people an opportunity to focus their attention.

I suggest that you start the music about ten or fifteen minutes before the meeting begins. Urge people to be on time, or better, to arrive five minutes or more before the official meeting time, so no one enters after the opening meditation has begun. Give each other the gift of silence so you can relax, gather yourselves together, and be present to each other and to God. I encourage people not to read during the quiet opening time—reading can be a distraction from focusing on being in the presence of God.

SEQUENCE

Each session is designed to follow the same sequence of events, one that enhances a meditative, prayerful reading and a reflective discussion:

Restful Beginning *(10 minutes)*

Each chapter begins with a meditation that focuses on the theme of the session and gradually leads toward a time of discussion. End the meditation with a song or prayer. Some suggestions are provided, including "Breathe in the Spirit," the theme song for this book (see p. 89). This song was written by Stephen Rush especially for *Catch Your Breath.* I am deeply grateful to him. (Dr. Rush is a professor of music at the University of Michigan in Ann Arbor, Michigan, a composer, pianist, and member of Campus Chapel where I serve as pastor.) After the closing song or prayer, you might well spend a few minutes talking about the theme of this meditation using the suggestions in the right margin.

Reviewing *(10 minutes)*

Let your discussion of the time of meditation lead to a review of your insights, questions, and experiences arising from the reading and at-home exercises you have been asked to do during the previous week. Being accountable to the group encourages you to do the suggested exercises or reflections during the week.

Reflecting *(30 minutes)*

This time of discussion is the heart of the session. Here you have a chance to talk together about how you react to the central ideas offered for your consideration.

Although your group is free to decide how they wish to read the materials offered, I suggest that for the maximum benefit each group member should read this chapter's contents early in the week. Or read it slowly throughout the week, taking time to reflect on the material and questions.

Read reflectively, thoughtfully, meditatively, even prayerfully. Take your time. Reading quickly the night before class will not give you enough opportunity to meditate on the material. You can't cram for sabbath time! You have to relax into it. Each chapter goes a little deeper into the topic and experience. Even though the book is short, it moves slowly. The questions, quotations, and exercises in the margin are there to slow you down and encourage you to reflect or pray as you read.

I encourage you to engage in a conversation with this book. Often I write in the margin of a book, engaging the author in dialogue. I would be pleased if you would use the margins (or a journal) to respond, question, affirm, comment on, or interact with what I have written.

These writings are meant to be evocative rather than the last word. If you don't particularly like an idea I present, throw it away. Don't argue with it; there is so much arguing going on today that I would rather we not add to it. Instead let's think and experience together on the way to understanding.

A reading may send you thinking in many other directions. A paragraph may be enough to contemplate in one sitting. An exercise or quotation may provide an incentive to pray or sing. I encourage slow reading rather than speed-reading so that you can savor what you read, but savor even more what you think and experience.

I hope your book is a mess when you finish—full of responses, prayers, meditative doodlings, maybe even drawings or poems or music. Your writing can be a travelogue of your journey through the book. Your notes will also provide you with insightful material to bring to the group discussions.

You may want to write in a notebook or journal rather than in the book. If you have kept a journal, you know what a valuable tool it is for recording the story of your inner journey. If you have not kept a journal, this might be a good time to begin. Writing your thoughts, questions, affirmations, feelings, insights, memories, dreams, and prayers can give you a record of how your spiritual life unfolds. A journal can help you befriend and integrate various parts of your life as you grow spiritually during the time you are reading this book—and beyond. (There are many books about journaling. I found helpful Morton Kelsey's *Adventure Inward: Christian Growth through Personal Journal Writing* and also "Journaling: Breathing Space in the Spiritual Journey," by Jan Johnson in *Weavings*, vol. VIII, number 2, March/April 1993.)

When you gather as a group, I also hope that you will spend your time together doing more than discussing or arguing about the written ideas. You don't risk much in doing that. I encourage you to bring your own prayerful responses to the readings and your own reflections on your practice as you try to develop a sabbath discipline that shapes your life and forms your piety. Any group discussion will be enhanced by your telling of your own experience of God's touch and sense of the presence of God's Spirit and God's grace in your life. In doing this you of course risk a lot (as Martin L. Smith observes in *A Season for the Spirit*). But you will also grow in your relationship as a group. You may want to remind and assist each other to keep the discussion focused on your reflections and prayers rather than on argument or debate.

May God bless and encourage you as you accept the divine gift of sabbath and dare to entrust your experiences to other pilgrims on the spiritual journey.

Sabbath Time *(10 minutes)*

This section is meant to help you gather up your thoughts and experiences and leave the session with a peaceful attitude. The exercise should begin about ten minutes before the scheduled end of the meeting.

A prayer or song will close your time together in a worshipful manner.

Home Alone

This study extends beyond the time you spend together in your group session. It provides exercises that can be used during the week to deepen the sabbath attitudes and practices you have learned during the sessions.

The purpose of this book is to help you gradually develop attitudes and practices that will continue long after the course is over. Hopefully, you will be attracted to a sabbath discipline that you can carry into every day of your life. So please take this part of the course seriously. It is probably the most important part! By the end of our time together we may be living a little more sabbath-like than we were before!

You may want to structure your time of personal reading and meditation along the lines of the structure of the chapters. This may set a pattern that will grow on you as you build a sabbath discipline. Also, as you do the readings and exercises at home, pay attention to the setting. Having a room in your home or a certain place in a room for your "sabbath space" can help you ease into the proper attitude for reading, reflection, and prayer.

Now,
O Lord,
calm me into a quietness
that heals
and listens,
and molds my longings
and passions,
my wounds
and wonderings
into a more holy
and human
shape.

—TED LODER, *GUERILLAS OF GRACE*,
©1984, LURAMEDIA, INC., SAN DIEGO, CALIFORNIA.
USED BY PERMISSION.

Prologue: Getting Acquainted

God graces us with rest; and, as we respond with
our gratitude, receiving the gift, we begin to
enter into that balanced life which is our destiny
as the people of a loving Creator.
—ELIZABETH J. CANHAM, *A REST REMAINING*, P. 26

I had a friend in college who smelled books! Whenever he got a new book he would open it and smell the pages. It was one way of getting acquainted with the book he was about to read.

How do you become acquainted with a book? Look through the table of contents? Look at pictures? Page through to see how it's structured? Smell it? Feel it? Read the last chapter so you know the conclusions? Just dive in?

Sometimes I have to read a book for a course or for information about a topic. It feels like an obligation. It takes me a while even to open the book. At other times I'm ambivalent, feeling unsure whether I'm ready for this new learning experience. Still other times I'm eager. Someone I respect has recommended the book to me. Or I have read this author before and look forward to another experience with her or him. Or I have had a longing to know something about a topic, or to be inspired, or entertained. Sometimes I approach a book with the anticipation of meeting a new friend.

What thoughts and feelings do you have as you begin this book? Do you welcome or fear being challenged in new spiritual directions?

I would like to introduce you to this little book as if I were introducing you to a new friend. Over the year or so that I have been writing it, it has become my friend. (Sometimes it seemed like an elusive friend, sometimes almost like an enemy!) It is a rather unassuming friend. It does not have a lot of original things to say— there are already many books on sabbath. (Some that

I consulted are mentioned in the bibliography so you can read more on this subject if you would like.)

This modest friend simply points the way to a topic, an experience, and a Person much greater than itself. It seeks to be a companion on your spiritual way, initiating a conversation that explores sabbath ideas and practices that could shape your life as you live in the presence of God. This friend wants to lure you into a more intimate and personal friendship with God. It invites you to know and experience the Person of God more deeply as you listen and respond to God's invitation to sabbath rest.

This book comes out of weakness—I'm not very accomplished at sabbath-keeping and living. Yet it is part of a journey into a space and time that fascinates me. I long for sabbath attitudes and practices—not only for myself but also for you. I realize how essential they are for our spiritual formation. So I offer you an invitation to join me on this holy journey.

Perhaps you have some interest in enhancing your spiritual life by exploring sabbath attitudes and practices, and that's why you picked up the book. I hope so. For then we can get on with our journey right away.

As we travel together we are participating in a conversation and journey with God that has been going on for thirty-five hundred years! We will be roaming around in an ancient practice that comes from an ancient text. But it is as contemporary as the latest stress management course or meditative technique.

The search for peace is in the air today. How often I hear people pleading for relief from stress, for freedom from the rat race, for time to relax, for quality time with family and friends, for opportunities to touch the deeper recesses of their hearts or to reach out to the needy. I am struck by the lengths people will go to find such peace and release.

I heard on the news that Japanese executives were flying to the States for relaxation, massage, good food, and meditation at a resort out West—for $500-plus per day! How ironic, when such meditation and relaxation are available right in Japan. On the other hand, people from the West are turning East (Harvey Cox, *Turning East*). They are attracted to Zen; they go to learn transcendental meditation or yoga, or simply to attend retreats or take cruises or vacations. Still others are beginning to probe the piety or spirituality of their own tradition.

I have done some of that in my spiritual search. But as I thought about those Japanese executives looking for something in the States that was available at home, it struck me that Jews and Christians also have a practice as near as our Bible, as close as our tradition, as available as the next ten minutes or weekend: the sabbath!

The sabbath is a gift from God given to humanity right from the beginning. An attitude waiting to be lived ever since Moses received the Ten Commandments and Jesus declared that the sabbath was made for us! A promise that unfolds the more we participate in it. A vacation with God planned from the beginning to be enjoyed into eternity.

What comes to mind when you hear the word "sabbath"?

When one of my friends was studying Jewish and Christian sabbath practices, she exclaimed, "I wish I could do that!" We can. To do it we need desire and discipline. Many folks have been on this sabbath journey before us. They can give us lots of help. We will engage them as we look at Scripture and other writings. They will invite us to follow Jesus. With Jesus we will reflect on some of the attitudes that underlie the sabbath. And we will be encouraged to put those attitudes into practice, so we can mature in our friendship with God.

My hope is that in this journey together we can catch some of the profound meaning of sabbath and begin enjoying sabbath moments—not just one special day each week, but at various times in our busy week, even if only for ten or twenty minutes at a time. It may become a cumulative habit. We may find ourselves liking it so much that we will gradually want more and more until sabbath times become a delicious component of the rhythm of our lives. And we will be glad to heed often God's invitation to sabbath rest.

Now that you have been introduced to this book-friend, I hope you are inspired not only to scan it, or sniff it, but to breathe it. I hope it makes you wish to take a deep breath of God's grace, available in sabbath practices, and to pray with an openness to God's Holy Breath, who gives us life and peace.

As you begin this book, hear Jesus' question to two would-be disciples: "What are you looking for?" You might read John 1:35-39 together and reflect on that question. Make some notes of your thoughts, so that you can refer to them as you go on in the study of this book.

1

Sabbath
as Mindfulness

The bell calls in the town
Where forebears cleared the shaded land
And brought high daylight down
To shine on field and trodden road.
I hear, but understand
Contrarily, and walk into the woods.
I leave labor and load,
Take up a different story.
I keep an inventory
Of wonders and of uncommercial goods.

—WENDELL BERRY, *SABBATHS*, P. 9. © 1987 BY WENDELL BERRY. REPRINTED BY PERMISSION OF NORTH POINT PRESS, A DIVISION OF FARRAR, STRALLS & GIROUX, INC.

Restful Beginning

Initiate a time of quiet by reading Psalm 37:7:

Be still before the LORD, and wait patiently for him.

Allow this text to lead you gradually into a quiet, relaxed space before God by shortening the text at each reading and savoring each line before going on to the next.

Be still before the LORD and wait patiently for him.
Be still before the LORD and wait patiently . . .
Be still before the LORD and wait . . .
Be still before the LORD . . .
Be still . . .
Be . . .

Or similarly, Psalm 46:10:

"Be still, and know that I am God!"
"Be still, and know that I am . . . "
"Be still, and know . . . "
"Be still . . . "
"Be . . . "

For about five minutes simply be in the presence of God.

You may want to close with the song, "Breathe in the Spirit" (see p. 89).

After closing, consider whether your spirit really longs to "be still before the Lord." When do you experience true quietness? How do you find it?

Reviewing

If you did not discuss the introductory chapter earlier, spend a few minutes talking about group members' reactions to it and their expectations for this book and your sessions together.

Reflecting

SABBATH REMINDERS

Six o'clock Saturday night and the church bell was ringing! An odd time for a church bell to ring. Odd, since nothing was happening in the church at that time. However, something was supposed to be happening at home.

My childhood home in Roseland, a suburb on the South Side of Chicago, was right across the alley from that church. We lived so close that I couldn't miss hearing the ringing of the bell. (So close that my mother could whisper to my dad during the Sunday morning service, "Henry, I think I forgot to turn the oven on for the roast." And during the next hymn Dad could make it home, turn on the oven, and be back in his place at the end of the pew! Everybody in church knew what was happening: "Anne forgot the roast again!")

Do you have childhood memories of church bells? Any special meaning for you?

There were two towers at the front of the church, a tall one and a short one (the architect must have used an unfinished European cathedral as his model). In the taller tower was a fine bell. Attached to it was a long rope that hung inside the church by the steps leading to the balcony. That was a real temptation for us kids. I often fantasized sneaking up the steps to the balcony and pulling that rope to ring the bell at some odd time during the service or during the week. Or swinging precariously on the rope over the open stairwell. But I never did.

It was the janitor's job (privilege!) to ring the bell. When my friend's dad became the janitor, I got my wish. Sometimes Ed's dad would ask Ed to ring the bell. And once in a while he'd invite me to go with him into that empty church to ring the bell at six o'clock on Saturday night.

GETTING READY

The ringing of the bell at this odd time was a reminder for everyone in the neighborhood that it was time. Time to get ready.

So we got ready. The kitchen floor had been mopped. We ate our Saturday night hamburgers and fried potatoes. We took a bath. Shined our shoes. Set out our clothes for the next day. My mother peeled the potatoes and snapped the beans we'd eat for Sunday dinner with that pot roast. We hardly ever went out on Saturday night. Dating on Saturday night was discouraged. We went to bed at a reasonable hour.

We were winding down and getting ready for Sunday—the Lord's Day. The bell was a reminder to "remember the sabbath day, and keep it holy" (Ex. 20:8). Our sabbath day was beginning. Sabbath means simply "to stop, to cease." It is a word about work. Halt! It is stop day—a time to "leave labor and load and take up a different story."

The bell rang at nine o'clock the next morning, a half hour before Sunday worship started. It rang again at nine-thirty when our family was sitting in the tenth pew on the right side of the church. (We always sat in the same pew. I thought we paid rent for it when the offering plate came by. It was the one under the stained-glass picture of a lamb with a pennant. Nobody ever explained the symbolism to me, but I was sure the lamb was cheering for the Chicago Cubs.)

"The Sabbath itself is a sanctuary which we build, *a sanctuary in time*." Think about this statement by Abraham Joshua Heschel.

SABBATH QUIET

We worshiped on the Sabbath, then we went to Sunday school. Since our family lived so close to the church, older relatives came over for coffee to talk and to wait for their kids to get out of class. Then home for dinner.

Even though the potatoes were peeled on Saturday night, it did seem like my mother worked pretty hard at making a big dinner on Sunday. And if company was coming, she worked even harder. Mothers and preachers seemed to have to work on Sunday. We had debates about who was allowed to work on Sunday— preachers, nurses, doctors, firefighters, police. Not people in restaurants! So we did not go out to eat on Sunday. I don't remember including mothers in the debate. But the rest of us certainly didn't do any work. Well, maybe we did the dishes.

The rest of Sunday afternoon we did very little. We ceased most activity. We were released from working. We didn't play ball or ride our bikes or swim. We didn't shop. In fact, many of the stores were closed on Sunday. We didn't work in the yard. We were freed from mowing the lawn, weeding the garden, pruning the trees and bushes. We could just enjoy sitting in the yard. We were discouraged from studying or doing homework. We could read (but not the Sunday newspaper), visit relatives, visit people in the nursing home—singing and handing out tracts. Sleep! Yes, we could sleep. Sleep was a favorite resting activity on Sunday afternoon. (I still have the habit!)

Our Sunday/sabbath was the pause that refreshed us. It was a gentle, relaxing day—even if it was somewhat boring. It helped us refocus our lives and turn our attention to family, friends, worship, God, the Bible, and to caring for other people.

The bell rang at 6:30 p.m. to remind us once more to get ready for worship. And again at 7:00 as the evening service began. We rounded out this special day with worship. I never was sure whether sabbath time was over after evening worship or later. I think it would have been helpful if there had been another bell to tell us that the sabbath celebration was finished.

There was a lot of visiting on Sunday evenings. I remember visiting often with relatives. One of the wonderful things we did was sing together, with Uncle Sam at the piano. Maybe sabbath was over when the last hymn was sung. A bell would have helped.

SABBATH BELLS

Those sabbath bells have remained with me to this day.

I was reminded of those bells when I was traveling in Zurich, Switzerland. Bells ring often there. On Sunday morning it seemed liked hundreds of bells filled the whole city, calling people to waken, to worship, to enjoy this special day.

Thich Nhat Hanh, a Vietnamese Buddhist monk, thinks it is fortunate that "there are church bells all over Europe." He says:

> *Whenever I give a lecture in Switzerland, I always make use of the church bells to practice mindfulness. When the bells ring, I stop talking, and all of us listen to the full sound of the bell. We enjoy it so much. (I think it is better than the lecture!) . . . One day in Berkeley, I proposed to professors and students at the University of California that every time the bell on the campus sounds, they should pause in order to breathe consciously. Everyone should take the time to enjoy being alive! We should not just be rushing around all day. We have to learn to really enjoy our church bells and our school bells. Bells are beautiful, and they can wake us up.*
> —PEACE IS EVERY STEP: THE PATH OF MINDFULNESS IN EVERYDAY LIFE, P. 19

For Hanh the bells recalled the temple bells of his Buddhist monastery, what he calls bells of mindfulness. "Every time we hear the bell, we stop talking, stop our thinking, and return to ourselves, breathing in and out, and smiling. Whatever we are doing, we

Respond to these words: "Every hour is unique and the only one given at the moment, exclusive and endlessly precious."
—ABRAHAM JOSHUA HESCHEL

The meaning of the Sabbath is to celebrate time rather than space. Six days a week we live under the tyranny of things of space; on the Sabbath we try to become attuned to holiness in time.
—ABRAHAM JOSHUA HESCHEL

pause for a moment and just enjoy our breathing," he says (*Peace Is Every Step*, p. 18). Those temple bells are a reminder for Buddhists to stop everything and refocus their lives and reorient their thinking, something like the church bells were for us in Roseland every Saturday and Sunday of my childhood.

I gain deeper insight into the significance of those childhood sabbath bells when I visit a Benedictine monastery. Bells ring at various times during the day. Bells tell the monks that it is time. Time to do what needs doing at that time. Bells awaken the monks at 3:00 a.m. Vigils is at 3:30 when the bell rings again. Then at 7:30 for Mass. And so on during the day, for seven times of worship and prayer as well as for meals. I spoke to the bell-ringer. I asked him how many times he rings the bell. He told me he always does it with a prayer. When the prayer is over, he is finished ringing. I wonder whether our janitor said a prayer during bell-ringing in Roseland?

Bells remind the monks not only to wake up, to pray, to worship, to eat, to sleep. They are a reminder of another quality of time. Receptive time. Reflective time. Refocusing time.

I was walking with a monk, Brother David Steindl-Rast, around the University of Michigan campus one day. The carillon in Burton Tower chimes every fifteen minutes. Whenever it rang, Brother David turned to me and quietly said, "Praise the Lord." It reminded him of his monastery bell. When it sounds he takes a moment to refocus his thoughts and life toward God: Praise the Lord. So every time the bell rang when he was signing books, lecturing, or just talking, we would turn to each other with a knowing look. Praise the Lord. Now when I'm on campus, I have a constant reminder to refocus on God.

A siren became such a reminder as Brother David and I were walking through the University of Michigan Arboretum. We heard a siren from an ambulance as it came toward the University hospital. Brother David stopped, crossed himself, and prayed

> It is one thing to race or be driven by the vicissitudes that menace life, and another thing to stand still and to embrace the presence of an eternal moment.
> —ABRAHAM JOSHUA HESCHEL

for the people who were suffering. A common, ordinary sound evoking a heartfelt response.

What could do that for us? How about the seat-belt buzzer? Or the wristwatch beep? Or the alarm clock awakening us to another unique day? Maybe the ringing of the telephone? We could let it ring a couple of times as we focus our attention. Or even a red light—instead of being a hindrance to our getting somewhere fast, we can use it as a reminder to be grateful for the present moment. The flashing of lights and ringing of bells at a railroad crossing can give us opportunity to relax for a few minutes and catch our breath as the train goes by. The singing of a bird can call us to stop and remember our Creator and the beauty in our life.

These bells of mindfulness, or sabbath bells, call us to catch our breath and to pay attention to the meaning of our lives and the core of our existence. I invite you to think of these short moments of reflection as mini-sabbaths. Times when you are able to have a sabbath kind of attitude, a sabbath quality of time. We need such a sabbath attitude in the achievement-oriented, production-driven busyness of our contemporary lives.

As we proceed together through this book, let's develop a form of sabbath observance that we can practice in our particular life circumstances, with our work or study schedule, family and friendship demands, professional and personal pressures, leisure and entertainment attractions. It's no longer possible to prescribe one way to keep the sabbath holy and wholly. Instead of that being an excuse for not practicing sabbath, it can be an incentive for us to develop attitudes and practices that are biblically rooted, theologically sound, and historically and experientially informed, as well as contemporary, challenging, spiritually satisfying, and God-glorifying. We can do this as individuals, as families, and as (church) communities. Such a practice will be a liv-

Are there sounds or sights that serve as bells of mindfulness for you? Something that brings to remembrance a different quality of time and reminds you to pause, enjoy the present, and center your attention on God—if only for a moment? Sabbath bells that remind you to take sabbath time?

ing expression of our beliefs about God and about God's invitation to sabbath rest.

Sabbath Time

If you took such an attitude about prayer into your week, you would have the beginning of a sabbath attitude. What would it take for you to incorporate such "tranquillity" into each day of your week?

At the close of the session, reflect on the following words from John Calvin concerning prayer:

> Do you wish to pray
> In God's temple? Pray in yourself.
> [In] secret prayer . . . Christ bids us
> Descend into our hearts
> With our whole thought,
> Promises us God will be near us
> In the affection of our hearts,
> Entempled in our bodies.
> Pray you may in other places too,
> But prayer is something secret,
> Lodged chiefly in the heart,
> Requiring tranquillity
> Far from all teeming cares.

—FORD LEWIS BATTLES, *THE PIETY OF JOHN CALVIN*, © 1978. USED BY PERMISSION.

Home Alone

Take five minutes a day for meditation:
- read Calvin's words as a beginning
- repeat the opening exercise, using Psalm 37 or 46

Also this week continue to pay attention to whatever are bells of mindfulness or sabbath bells for you—sights, sounds, people, or events that remind you to take sabbath time, to focus your attention on God, to give praise to God. You may want to write them down and share them with the group in your next session.

Finally, read reflectively chapter 2, "Sabbath as Rest."

Sabbath
as Rest

"Come to me, all you that are weary and are carrying heavy burdens, and I will give you rest."

—MATTHEW 11:28

Restful Beginning

Begin a time of silence by reading Jesus' invitation written above.

Hear this as a personal invitation. Listen to it with your ears, mind, and heart. Reflect on it for about five minutes.

End the silence with the words of this song, spoken as a prayer:

> *I heard the voice of Jesus say, "Come unto me and rest; lay down, O weary one, lay down your head upon my breast."*
>
> *I came to Jesus as I was, so weary, worn, and sad; I found in him a resting place, and he has made me glad.*
>
> —HORATIUS BONAR

Conclude with the theme song: "Breathe in the Spirit."

After the silence, discuss how this invitation sounds to you. What do you think, feel, or experience as you hear it? How would you like to respond?

Reviewing

Review the group's experiences with the suggested five minutes a day for meditation. Did you find it calming, refreshing? Were you able to find bells of mindfulness or sabbath bells that enabled you to focus your attention on God?

Reflecting

REST

We all do it already—almost intuitively. We work and we rest. We produce and we play. We cram for an exam, and afterward we celebrate. We achieve, but then we find ways to escape: a movie, a concert,

What is the typical
pattern of your day or
week? How do you
relax? Do you find
relaxing difficult?
Wasteful? Guilt produc-
ing? Beneficial?
Invigorating?

woodworking, baking, gardening, tennis, jogging, swimming. We labor and then try to find opportunities for leisure—a day off, a vacation—so we can get recharged and return to work refreshed. And if we don't take some time off but just keep on working, we get so exhausted that our body reacts. We become so fatigued that we have to take a nap. Or we get sick and are forced to stop.

We seem to recognize intuitively the work/rest rhythm as a basic human need. Our basic life-rhythm involves taking hold and letting go, production and refreshment, work and rest. In our society we often emphasize the side of production, activity, and work and then complain about burnout and stress. To relieve the stress, we go on escape weekends. Or maybe we do mindless activity that is supposed to recharge us for work.

Work is often our primary category, so even our leisure has to be productive. Some folk are afraid to take even short periods of time off because of competition on the job. They take along their briefcases and laptop computers and have a "working vacation." That sounds like a contradiction to me.

You probably know people who don't take time off and think they are really dedicated people. I know a church executive who spoke with pride about not taking a vacation for five years. Sometimes I find myself so occupied in teaching people about prayer, solitude, meditation, and sabbath-keeping, that I hardly find time to relax or pray! That is a contradiction for me.

How is not finding
enough time for rest
unnatural? Unspiritual?

And it's unnatural. It's not just unspiritual but unnatural not to have time for rest. It's unhealthy not to have a rhythm of work and rest, activity and receptivity. For this is the rhythm of creation right from the beginning: "On the seventh day God finished the work that he had done, and he rested on the seventh day from all the work that he had done. So God blessed the seventh day and hallowed it, because on it God rested from all the work that he had done in creation" (Gen. 2:2-3). God took a break, like an artist stepping back from her easel and admiring her painting. God took a breather, like a weary factory laborer stepping out for some fresh air.

And we are invited to do the same.

SABBATH INVITATION

Isn't it soothing to hear Jesus say, "Come off by yourselves; let's take a break and get a little rest"? Especially since Jesus and his harried disciples seem to be in a predicament similar to ours: "There was constant coming and going. They didn't even have time to eat" (Mark 6:36, *The Message).* And no fast-food restaurants! How contemporary. How sad.

Jesus lived an active life. People made constant demands on him. Even when "he went home . . . the crowd came together again, so that they could not even eat. When his family heard it, they went out to restrain him, for people were saying, 'He has gone out of his mind'" (Mark 3:20-21). In the middle of such a busy life Jesus somehow found opportunity to get away from the pressures and to be alone, to pray, to spend time with God, to gain perspective, to be renewed, to regenerate his energy and that of his followers.

Jesus' invitation comes as a welcome relief to frazzled, preoccupied people: "Come to me, all you that are weary and are carrying heavy burdens, and I will give you *rest*" (Matt. 11:28). The invitation is even more compelling in Eugene Peterson's translation: "Are you tired? Worn out? Burned out . . . ? Come to me. Get away with me and you'll recover your life. I'll show you how to take a real rest. Walk with me and work with me—watch how I do it. Learn the unforced rhythms of grace" (*The Message*).

The very words instill tranquillity: "Learn from me . . . and you will find *rest for your souls.*" Just what we need but find so elusive.

> **Could McDonald's advertising slogan "Have you had a break today?" become a spiritual question reminding you of Jesus' invitation?**

> **Perfect rest is an art. It is the result of an accord of body, mind and imagination.**
> —ABRAHAM
> JOSHUA HESCHEL

I found such rest in an unexpected place one day—on the main shopping street in Holland, Michigan. At the corner of 8th and Central there is a small park with a sculpture of chamber musicians. While my wife was shopping, I sat on a bench by the sculpture, amid flowers and evergreens, and listened to the classical music being played. I wonder how many take advantage of that invitation to sabbath on a busy street? A woman stopped long enough for a cigarette. A young fellow stopped for a few minutes while waiting for someone. I was able to stay for half an hour of quiet. I found rest for my body—and soul. It was like the divine invitation: "Come to me. . . . "

In Jesus' words we can hear an echo of the fourth commandment: "Remember the sabbath day, and keep it holy. Six days you shall labor and do all your work. But the seventh day is a sabbath to the LORD your God; you shall not do any work. . . . For in six days the LORD made heaven and earth, the sea, and all that is in them, but rested the seventh day" (Ex. 20:8-11).

God's invitation to sabbath rest is an invitation to peace in the middle of feverish activity. A law that protects our free time! A practice that comes from before the fall of humankind into sin. It is a God-practiced and God-given rhythm woven into the fabric of human life. It urges us to imitate the divine rhythm: Remember the stop day to keep it holy—and rest. Like God, work and then stop to rest.

Stopping and *resting* are two key attitudes and practices that might help us shape our ordinary lives.

THE STOP DAY

"Remember the sabbath day" is a word about work. There is nothing wrong with work. It is one necessary component of the divine rhythm. Yet we often give work the strongest emphasis in the rhythm. *Sabbath* emphasizes the second part. Sabbath was (and is) a time to cease all activity in which one was gainfully employed and simply acknowledge the goodness of creation and life. It is a certain kind of consciousness. It is an opportunity to affirm and enjoy what is, to be mindful and attentive.

A time to enjoy God, to be mindful of the presence of and our relationship with God. Sabbath is an opportunity to gain perspective, to remember that our lives have a focus and a purpose larger than our day-to-day activity. We realize that we are important as human beings created in the image of God and not just for our usefulness, our productivity.

When we cease from work, we show ourselves to be labor's master. Like God on the seventh day of creation, we can look back and say, "I rule my work, my work doesn't rule me." For a period of time we can say "I'm finished." Even when our work is not complete, we can say, "I'm done."

When sundown comes on Friday night, a rabbi friend of mine says, "I'm finished." Even when there are books piled high to read, a lawn to mow, bills to pay, groceries to buy, people to see, and a world to care about. He is imitating God in the Genesis story: "On the seventh day God finished the work that he had done, and he rested on the seventh day from all the work that he had done." Now obviously, says the rabbi, God was not done with creation. It had only begun. It is still going on. But on the seventh day it seems that God says, "I am done. Whatever is done is done. Now I stop. My work does not rule me. I rule my work. I can take a break."

Sabbath time is time when we imitate God by stopping our work and resting.

In her book *Keeping the Sabbath Day Wholly*, Marva Dawn expands the idea of ceasing to include ceasing work, ceasing accomplishments, ceasing worry, ceasing possessiveness, ceasing being possessed by our culture, and ceasing the mundane (pp. 3-50). If we can stop all this for a day, or even for mini-sabbaths during each day, we may have touched something deep that can shape our lives in the divine pattern given for our pleasure and our total health.

> Does not our work always remain incomplete? What the verse means to convey is: Rest on the Sabbath as if all your work were done. Another interpretation: *Rest even from the thought of labor.*
>
> —ABRAHAM JOSHUA HESCHEL

> There are places [one] can go, a scene [one] can create, a haven for [one's] heart. The reason they seem scarce is that no one wants them; there is a small demand. But lovers always manage to find a place to go where they can be alone for a while. So can you.
>
> —MATTHEW KELTY

As attractive as stopping and resting may be, it is not easy. When I was exploring sabbath in some sermons, a parishioner remarked, "I tried doing sabbath last Sunday afternoon. I stopped working and just rested. It was one of the worst times of my life! For a day to be worthwhile I have to do at least one productive thing." Sabbath rest may seem wasteful for Calvinists taught never to waste time!

There is a sentence that keeps coming back to me whenever I take time off: "Time marches on. Let's try to keep up with it." It was the favorite line of one of my Christian grade-school teachers. Anyone who fooled around in class or was disruptive had to stay after school and "write lines." I remember writing that line five hundred times. The thousand times or more I wrote it during the year seemed like a waste of time to me. But that line still haunts me when I try to take time for sabbath solitude, silence, and rest.

Another person in the congregation said, "For me taking time for rest is like getting a kink in the hose when I'm watering the lawn. If I don't get the kink out, the pressure will build up so much that the hose will explode!" Life flows when there is activity.

However, real life flows even better when there is a natural rhythm of activity and rest. Marva Dawn encourages us to observe a sabbath that includes spiritual rest, physical rest, emotional rest, intellectual rest, and social rest. "Fundamental to it all is the true resting in God's grace that sets us free" (*Keeping the Sabbath Wholly*, p. 97). It is a rhythm of grace. Jesus invites us to learn "the unforced rhythms of grace." To get away with him, catch our breath, and recover our life.

Sabbath Time

Five or more minutes before the end of the session, bring the discussion to a close and begin a time of quiet. Repeat the meditation with which the session began. Listen once more to Jesus' invitation, "Are you tired? Worn out? Burned out . . . ? Come to me. Get away with me and you'll recover your life. I'll show you how to take a real rest. Walk with me and work with me—watch how I do it. Learn the unforced rhythms of grace" (Matt. 11:28-29, *The Message*).

Hear also the commandment to stop and rest.

Close with a prayer of thanks for the invitation and for the courage to respond to it in the coming week. You may want to end with some meditative music or by singing "Breathe in the Spirit."

Home Alone

Repeat the following spiritual exercise during this coming week. Spend about ten minutes being with Jesus each day. Don't do anything special. Just be together at his invitation.

End your time each day with the words of the hymn:

> *I heard the voice of Jesus say, "Come unto me and rest; lay down, O weary one, lay down your head upon my breast."*
>
> *I came to Jesus as I was, so weary, worn, and sad; I found in him a resting place, and he has made me glad.*
> —HORATIUS BONAR

Fill in the third and fourth lines with how you came to Jesus each time and what he does for you:

I came to Jesus as I was, so _____,

_____, and _____;

I found in him _____, and

he has made me _____.

Notice your response to Jesus' invitation on various days or at various times during the day. Record them in your journal.

Finally, read and reflect meditatively and prayerfully on chapter 3, "Sabbath as Refreshment."

3

Sabbath
as Refreshment

The Lord God formed man from the dust of the ground, and breathed into his nostrils the breath of life; and the man became a living being.

—GENESIS 2:7

[Jesus] breathed on [his disciples] and said to them, "Receive the Holy Spirit."

—JOHN 20:22

Restful Beginning

Begin your time of silent meditation by reading Jesus' Easter evening words to his disciples:

When it was evening on that day, the first day of the week . . . Jesus came and stood among [the disciples] and said, "Peace be with you." After he said this, he showed them his hands and his side. . . . [Jesus] breathed on them and said to them, "Receive the Holy Spirit."

—JOHN 20:19-22

Imagine that you are present with Jesus' disciples. Jesus' words, "Peace be with you" and "Receive the Holy Spirit," are spoken to you. What is your response?

Let these words lead you into five minutes of silent reflection and meditation.

End the silence by singing "Breathe in the Spirit." Remember to sing it over a number of times. (You will find this theme song printed in the back of this book. Since it will be suggested often, you might take the time now to learn it together.)

Reviewing

Talk together about your experience with the opening meditation and with the meditative exercises suggested for the past week. What insights did you gain? When did God seem present—or absent? Did anything else happen to you? Did you remember to listen for bells of mindfulness?

Let your responses lead into the discussion that follows about the concept and experience of sabbath as a time to take a deep breath.

Reflecting

THE BREATH OF LIFE

Describe an experience of being breathless— from running or giving birth or having surgery or being ill. Did you sense in a new way the relationship between breath and life?

Breathing is so natural and automatic that we hardly notice it. It's easy to take our breath for granted until we run for a bus, just make it, and flop into a seat to catch our breath. Then we become conscious of what we do so naturally most of the time—breathe.

As I watched runners coming in from a 5K race, I was reminded of how important breathing is. They came past the finish line, through the chute, and then bent over, panting, gasping for breath. The runners realized how essential breath was. They did not take it for granted. They needed every bit of air they could gasp!

When we exert ourselves, it's as if our breath gets away from us and we have to grab it back again to renew our vitality. After working in the garden or playing tennis, we realize we need a *breather*. Or we come home tired at the end of a busy day and need to *catch our breath*.

During childbirth a mother is continually encouraged in her breathing. There are different breath patterns for various parts of labor. Breathing is part of the birth process. When the baby is born, we immediately make sure it is breathing. Where there's breath, there's life. How vital breath is! Without it we die.

Breath is also necessary for our spiritual lives. Without the Breath of God we die spiritually. We just don't notice that as quickly.

Physical and spiritual breath come together in the Genesis story of the creation of human beings. God formed a human being out of earth. But it was simply inanimate until God breathed into the nostrils the breath of life—and then it became a living being! We humans are God-animated beings. The Breath of the living God becomes our breath! That breath is

> **Every breath we draw is a gift of God's love, every moment of existence is a grace, for it brings with it immense graces from Him. Gratitude therefore takes nothing for granted.**
>
> —THOMAS MERTON

the primal source of life. It got us going in the beginning and has kept us going ever since. We are breathing beings.

THE BREATH THAT REFRESHES

Sabbath is an invitation to catch our breath physically and spiritually. In this we continue to imitate God.

Exodus 31 presents us with an extraordinary picture of God: "In six days the LORD made heaven and earth, and on the seventh day [God] rested, and was refreshed" (Ex. 31:17). The writer seems to be elaborating on Genesis 2:3: "God rested from all the work that he had done in creation." In Exodus the idea of God's *being refreshed* defines and expands the idea of God *resting*.

Maybe this means simply that God relaxed, as we relax after exerting ourselves. But it may also be saying something deeper about breath as a primal source of life. The phrase *was refreshed* is used only a couple of times in the Hebrew Scriptures, and each time it speaks of an exhausted person's energy being restored. It's like a battery being recharged. After King David fled from his son Absalom, we read, "The king and all the people who were with him arrived weary at the Jordan; and there he refreshed himself" (2 Sam. 16:14). They arrived there dead-tired but were revived. They got back their life, their *nephesh* or soul-life. The Hebrew carries the idea that when we are exhausted, we lose our identity, our soul. As we sometimes say, "I'm just not myself." When refreshed, we get that identity back and are re-souled.

A Jewish friend told me that whenever his family reads Exodus 31:17, they take a deep breath between "rested" and "was refreshed." It is a way to experience and remember the text.

The sabbath is not only for stopping and resting, but for being refreshed. It is the day we get back our identity, our soul. It is for catching our breath and coming alive again!

> What do you think of the idea that God wants or seeks refreshment?

> Every seventh day a miracle comes to pass, the resurrection of the soul, of the soul of man and of the soul of all things. A medieval sage declares: The world which was created in six days was a world without a soul. It was on the seventh day that the world was given a soul.
> —ABRAHAM JOSHUA HESCHEL

God, who is our inspiration, invites us to tap that source of renewal: "Six days you shall do your work, but on the seventh day you shall rest, so that . . . [you] may be refreshed" (Ex. 23:12). Sabbath is the pause that refreshes.

We imitate God in taking a sabbath break not only to stop and to rest, but also to catch our breath. And in doing that, we may catch the Holy Breath of God.

In many religious traditions, breath is a primary image for the divine presence with and within us. In Christianity, it's one of the images for our receiving the Holy Spirit. John Calvin says "to speak of God as Spirit is to speak in the most immanent and immediate way of God's presence. It is the mystery of God, as close to us as our very breath" (Ford L. Battles, *The Piety of John Calvin*). Perhaps the Holy Spirit could be called the Holy Breath, the Holy Breathing, or the Breath of God. As Edwin Hatch phrases it in his well-known hymn:

> *Breathe on me, Breath of God, fill me with life anew, that I may love the way you love, and do what you would do.*

Lawrence Kushner says that when the High Priest entered the holy of holies on Yom Kippur, he "had to do only one thing . . . utter . . . the ineffable four-letter Name of God. *Yod, Hey, Vay, Hey.* It is a name made from the three letters of the Hebrew alphabet that function primarily as vowels. . . . The reason that God's Name is unpronounceable is because the Name of Being is the sound of breathing. The High Priest went into the innermost sanctuary and simply breathed" (*GOD was in this PLACE & I, i did not know*, pp. 96-97).

Jesus' actions and words on Easter evening make this most vivid. He came into a locked room and greeted his friends: "Peace be with you." And when he had said this, he breathed on them (like God breathing the breath of life into the first human) and said: "Receive the Holy Spirit" (John 20:22). This is a Pentecost experience on Easter evening. The risen

Does calling the Holy Spirit the Breath of God or Holy Breath help you to a greater sense of the intimacy of God with you and within you?

Christ transmitting Holy Breath to his followers. The Spirit that breathed into creation, into prophets, into Mary, now was breathed into the disciples and the church. They came alive with the life of God.

That Spirit/Breath is available for us! "Breath is always with us. Remembering the breath, returning to the breath, becomes a way of remembering and returning to the present and to the presence of God" (Diana Eck, *Encountering God,* p. 127).

REMEMBERING YOUR BREATH

I was at the dentist getting a gold crown. While taking an impression, she said I would have to sit for six minutes while the stuff was in my mouth. "Do you want something to read?" she asked. "No," I answered, "I'll just breathe. I'll take a mini-sabbath and focus on God." And I did. It was refreshing.

Remembering our breath is one of the simplest ways of becoming aware of God. So various forms of meditation encourage us to be conscious of our breathing. The practice is very simple, though not easy. Concentrate on breathing in and breathing out. Such "resting the mind on the breath for a sustained period of meditation or for a moment virtually any time of the day [can be] a vehicle for resting in the Spirit. It is a vehicle for returning attention to the moment and for returning attention to God" (Diana Eck, *Encountering God,* p. 127).

There is a stoplight at the intersection of Hill and Main streets in Ann Arbor. It remains red for sixty-seven seconds. I know. While waiting for it to change to green, I used to count the seconds and become more and more irritated. But now I breathe and refocus my attention. I let the stoplight be a call to a mini-sabbath and to prayer.

Such a practice of brief meditations might help us rediscover the treasure we already have as Jews and Christians—the sabbath! It might be encouraging for Christians, who have found Eastern meditation beneficial but feel they cannot accept the conceptual

Stop for a minute or two and simply be aware of your breathing in and out. How relaxing and refreshing that is! Take a mini-sabbath to refocus your life toward God.

Reflect on how you might develop a sabbath attitude of stopping, resting, and catching your breath.

background that underlies it, to realize that there is something similar in our own tradition. "The spirit of the Sabbath is a biblical equivalent of meditation. It nurtures the same kind of awareness that meditation nurtures. It is a particular form of consciousness, a way of being and thinking that strongly resembles what Buddhists call 'mindfulness'" (Harvey Cox, *Turning East*, p. 69).

Mini-sabbaths of meditation in which we concentrate on our breathing can be one way to foster awareness of our vital connection with God. Whether they last for two minutes or twenty, mini-sabbaths can make us gradually aware of God's Spirit breathing in the daily experiences of our lives.

I needed some physical therapy for my shoulders. Each therapy session began with lying down for twenty minutes with a heating pad on each shoulder. A time when I could do very little. What an opportunity! I had permission to be quiet and breathe for twenty minutes, to do holy breathing with a focus on the Divine Presence. Soon the assistant who brought the heat would say, "Time to meditate." I had a built-in sabbath time every other day!

I like to think of sabbath as Holy Breathing Time. And if we as Christians celebrate Sunday as a sabbath day, we can celebrate not only the resurrection of Jesus on the first day of the week, but also recall that on Easter evening the risen Jesus breathed the Holy Spirit. We could call it Holy Breathing Day, or Catch Your Breath Day. We could use sabbath times as opportunities to be gratefully conscious of inhaling God's creative and recreative power—as a creation and a Pentecost experience.

In the tempestuous ocean of time and toil there are islands of stillness where man may enter a harbor and reclaim his dignity. The island is the seventh day, the Sabbath, a day of detachments from things, instruments and practical affairs as well as attachment to the spirit.

—ABRAHAM JOSHUA HESCHEL

A SABBATH RHYTHM

Being active all the time is like exhaling all the time. Breathing out is necessary, of course. Productivity is important. Achievement can be fulfilling. Work is also a gift. Activity keeps life interesting. Parker Palmer is helpful:

> For some of us, the primary path to aliveness is the active life [of work, creativity, and caring. The active life is] an extraordinary mix of blessing and curse. The blessing is obvious . . . . : the active life makes it possible to discover ourselves and our world, to test and extend our powers, to connect with other beings, to co-create a common reality. . . . Take away the opportunity to work, to create, or to care . . . and you have deprived someone of a chance to feel fully human.

> But the active life also carries a curse. Many of us know what it is to live lives not of action but of frenzy, to go from day to day exhausted and unfulfilled by our attempts to work, create, and care. Many of us know the violence of active life. . . . Action poses some of our deepest spiritual crises as well as some of our most heartfelt joys.
> —PARKER PALMER, THE ACTIVE LIFE: A SPIRITUALITY OF WORK, CREATIVITY, AND CARING, PP. 9-11

Activity is as important as exhaling. But we need to alternate it with inhaling. Unless we are willing to release the air we hold in our lungs, there can never be a new breath or continued life. Sabbath is for catching a new breath—breathing deeply so that we can live physically and spiritually.

Once we catch on to the value of taking a sabbath breather, we can encourage our pressured, hassled, production-orientated, exhausted society to take a deep breath and realize that we are God-animated people.

Exhale continually as you read this paragraph. Could you do it? How did it feel to breath in again?

A small wooden flute,
an empty, hollow reed,
rests in her silent hand.

it awaits the breath
of one who creates song
through its open form.

my often-empty life
rests in the hand of God;
like the hollowed flute,
it yearns for the melody
which only Breath can give.

the small, wooden flute and I,
we need the one who breathes,
we await one who makes melody.

and the one whose touch creates,
awaits our empty, ordinary forms,
so that the song-starved world
may be fed with golden melodies.

—JOYCE RUPP, "INSTRUMENTS OF GOD," *MAY
I HAVE THIS DANCE.* © 1992 BY AVE MARIA PRESS,
NOTRE DAME, IN 46556. USED BY PERMISSION.

Sabbath Time

Reflect on these words:

*The church has a two-thousand year tradition of
associating breath with prayer. [Since Jesus breathed on
the disciples and said] "Receive the Holy Spirit," and
they breathed in. . . . And [when] Jesus breathed his
last, his last words were, "Father, into Thy hands I
commit my spirit"—words of complete surrender.
For those of us wanting to surrender at deeper and
deeper levels to God's grace, breathing out is a way of
prayer. Some will couple the breath with the words of
Jesus, "Into Thy hands." Then breathing in and
breathing out becomes a prayer of receiving and
giving. . . . Our prayer may become as close to us as
our breath. God is!*

—JOHN ACKERMAN, FROM "HOLY BREATH," A LEAFLET
PRINTED BY WESTMINSTER PRESBYTERIAN CHURCH,
MINNEAPOLIS, MN 55403

Take five minutes for meditative prayer. Close your eyes, be silent, and breathe. Breathing in, hear words from God: "Receive the Holy Spirit." Breathing out, say words to God: "Into your hands" or "Into your hands I commit my spirit."

You might close by saying the familiar words

> Breathe on me, Breath of God, fill me with life anew, that I may love the way you love, and do what you would do.

Then sing "Breathe in the Spirit."

Home Alone

Take five minutes each day to be aware of breathing in and out, accompanying that action with the words that you used at the close of this session.

Read and reflect thoughtfully on chapter 4, "Sabbath as Receptivity."

4

Sabbath as Receptivity

"I am the Lord your God, who brought you up out of the land of Egypt. Open your mouth wide and I will fill it."

—PSALM 81:10

Restful Beginning

Begin by reading Psalm 23 (especially 1-3a) slowly and meditatively, using one or more of the versions that follow. Let these words lead you into a few minutes of silent reflection and meditation on resting with God.

> *He makes me lie down in green pastures,*
> *he leads me beside quiet waters,*
> *he restores my soul. (NIV)*

> *Fresh and green are the pastures*
> *where he gives me repose.*
> *Near restful waters he leads me,*
> *to revive my drooping spirit. (The Psalms, A New Translation)*

> *Lord, my shepherd, there's nothing I lack.*
> *In fresh pastures you let me lie down;*
> *You lead me beside quiet waters;*
> *You restore me to life. (The Psalms, A New Translation for Prayer and Worship)*

End with a prayer based on Psalm 23:1-3 and by singing "Breathe in the Spirit."

Reviewing

Talk about your experience this past week with being aware of breathing in and out and connecting that with the Holy Breath of God.

Consider how Psalm 23 invites us to sabbath rest as it describes "the waters of *stillness*" (v. 2). Heschel helps us understand the rich meaning of *menuha*, the Hebrew word it uses:

After the six days of creation—what did the universe still lack? *Menuha.* Came the Sabbath, came *menuha*, and the universe was complete.
—ABRAHAM JOSHUA HESCHEL

So how does Heschel define this rest?

It is the state wherein man lies still, wherein the wicked cease from troubling and the weary are at rest.
—ABRAHAM JOSHUA HESCHEL

Reflecting

RECEIVING IS GRACE

When we concentrate on our breathing, we can understand and experience a little more clearly that the Christian life begins with receiving. First, receiving the life-giving air we breathe. Second, simply taking in and receiving the life-sustaining Breath of God. We do nothing to acquire it. The Breath of God is given, and we simply receive it as a gift.

What do you think of this idea that we are receivers? How does it make you feel?

According to the Genesis story, humanity began with God's activity—breathing into Adam's nostrils the breath of life. We still receive life from the Creator of the universe. We receive new life from our risen, Spirit-sending Savior. We receive inspiration and strength to live this new life from the Holy Spirit. God is the Giver. We are, first of all, receivers.

This is the radical good news of God's grace. We are accepted and beloved by God before we do anything! A Reformed spirituality begins with this understanding and this experience of grace. It begins with grace, not achievement; pardon, not guilt; forgiveness, not confession; justification, not faith; freedom, not fear; God's original love, not our original sin. It begins with receiving, not giving.

Grace was there right at the beginning. Adam was created at the end of the creation week and began the first full day of life on the sabbath, on the day that God rested! Before achieving anything, Adam had a day of rest and shared with God a time of refreshment. It was a time for receiving. A day of grace.

RECEIVING TIME

Sabbath is a day of grace, a time for receiving. The creation rhythm alternates between activity and receptivity. Sabbath is "a practice of receptive time that both balances and permeates our active time. . . . a different quality of time from the daily routine of our lives so that we may recognize and live out our full humanity" (Tilden Edwards, *Sabbath Time,* p. 8). It is a time "in which being replaces doing," and affirming takes precedence over accumulation (Harvey Cox, *Turning East,* p. 72).

The gracious invitation "I am the LORD your God, who brought you up out of the land of Egypt. Open your mouth wide and I will fill it" was literally fulfilled when God provided the Jews a white, sweet substance to eat during their forty-year sojourn in the wilderness. It was called *manna,* which means *What is it?* Every morning for six days of the week the Israelites gathered and ate "What Is It?" breakfast food. Any that was left over until the next day spoiled.

Except on the seventh day! On the sixth day, the people were supposed to gather enough manna for two days, so they would not have to work on the seventh day. What was left over for the seventh day did not spoil. Moses said, "'Six days you shall gather it; but on the seventh day, which is a sabbath, there will be none.' On the seventh day some of the people went out to gather, and they found none" (Ex. 16:26-27). They could not work gathering food for there was none to gather! "So the people rested on the seventh day" (v. 30). This is sabbath observance even before the fourth commandment is given! A reminder that the Lord provides and God's people receive. "Open your mouth wide and I will fill it."

Sabbath is a gift from God that we are invited to receive. It seems that on the sabbath it is better to receive than to give.

I find it helpful to think of sabbath rest as a time of receptivity rather than simply inactivity. We are involved in receptivity. We can be fully present to what is, affirming it. We enjoy and appreciate creation rather than fix it. We savor the gifts God has given us. We receive life from God, our creator, savior, sustainer, healer. We appreciate the giftedness of life, of nature, of other people, of ourselves. We pay atten-

Imagine coming to work and finding a sign on the door: "No work today; no opportunity to accumulate. Instead, receive." How would you react?

Stop a moment. Relax into an attitude of receptivity, with your hands on your lap, palms up and open. Open your mind and heart as well. Think of the gifts you have received today, this week. Simply realize that you are a gifted person.

tion to what is around us, in us, and beyond us. We are attentive to our relationship with our Divine Friend.

PAYING ATTENTION

A rabbi friend of mine says that the sabbath day is a day for paying attention to life, for opening up to the moment and gaining a new awareness.

Others have noted that being aware, conscious, mindful, observant, alert, attentive is a primary spiritual attitude:

> *Meditation is one of the ways in which the spiritual [person] keeps awake!*
> —THOMAS MERTON, *THOUGHTS IN SOLITUDE*, P. 47

> *Staying awake and keeping watch is a serious and difficult spiritual discipline, especially for people of action. . . . [In Gethsemane], when Jesus asked his disciples to "stay awake and pray," [he] was not calling them to heroic action; he was not asking them to do anything at all. He was calling them to simple attention, watchfulness, and that was infinitely more difficult. . . . Developing the capacity for stable attention is the most important of spiritual arts. As a nineteenth-century Russian Orthodox teacher put it, "Without attention there is no prayer."*
> —DIANA ECK, *ENCOUNTERING GOD*, PP. 145-147

Who or what do you think of when you hear the word "contemplation"? Do you think of it as paying attention?

Paying attention is an attitude and practice of contemplation. Sabbath gives us the opportunity to develop contemplative attitudes toward life.

Some suppose that contemplation belongs in a monastery or is reserved for supremely religious folk uninvolved in the demands that swamp our lives. But contemplation is an attitude and practice anyone can have. It can celebrate the way God's Spirit breathes in the daily experiences of life, so that ordinary people like us are sustained by the knowledge of God's presence (William Calahan, *Noisy Contemplation*, p. 1). Contemplation can be a way we live our ordinary lives in a deep way even when they are active, noisy, and practical. It requires no more time but rather a different perspective.

Contemplation means being observant and focused, mindful and receptive. In short, a contemplative person pays attention.

Most of us have the tools to pay attention: our outer senses (eyes, ears, touch, smell, taste) and our inner senses (intuition, compassion, imagination, memory, thinking). We already know how to do it.

We contemplate babies. We watch every move and ooh and aah in wonder at each sound and gesture. I remember my three-month-old granddaughter lying on my chest. We just looked at each other, communicating with eyes and smiles. We stayed like that for half an hour. I was completely captivated by her. I wish I were that focused during prayer!

In the fall of 1995, I saw people similarly engrossed at a stunning exhibit of paintings by Claude Monet at the Art Institute in Chicago. In the last room of the exhibit a hush came over the crowd. People were speechless as they viewed huge canvasses of water lilies. As people sat to contemplate the wonder of it all, it seemed as peaceful as a church or meditation hall. One of Monet's ideals was such *visual meditation*.

I observed another crowd of contemplatives in Yellowstone National Park. They were standing or sitting on benches waiting, some as long as an hour, for Old Faithful to erupt, waiting to see this one minute of nature's extravagance. And then it happened! All oohs and aahs and cheers. People forgetting themselves, all focused on this one act of God in nature. Absorbed. Contemplatives! They may not have known they were praying. Too bad. This paying attention with awe and wonder, the oohs and aahs of admiration, is prayer and a mini-sabbath of contemplation.

Sabbath is a day and a time to cultivate contemplation, to understand the *aah* of things, to pay attention to God's creation. We can develop a sabbath attitude simply by looking around us every day with conscious admiration and appreciation. There are bells of mindfulness, sabbath reminders, everywhere.

Recall a time when you were so absorbed by something (a sight, sound, experience, book, Scripture) that you hardly thought of anything else. That's the beginning of contemplation!

Consider these words from the Belgic Confession: The "universe is before our eyes like a beautiful book in which all creatures, great and small, are as letters to make us ponder the invisible things of God: his eternal power and his divinity."
—ARTICLE 2

EATING MINDFULLY

Visiting a monastery I learned to meditate during prayer. But I also learned to work meditatively in the garden and in the kitchen preparing food. And then to eat mindfully.

We eat every day. So eating mindfully can become a daily practice of meditation. Yet many of our meals are eaten while reading the paper, watching TV, listening to the radio, or doing business. The food is almost forgotten in the process. At business lunches the meal is almost incidental. After such meals I hardly remember what I ate.

Eating mindfully can bring you back to the present moment and help you savor the meal itself. Before eating, contemplate the food; then eat it with awareness.

Christians have a tradition of offering a prayer of gratitude before the meal. That practice can make us more mindful in our eating. However, the prayers are often not connected with the meal itself but include many other things. That's fine. But we can also learn to pray the meal itself. In a sense we already do that without calling it prayer. We say, "That looks great," or "Wow, this is delicious," or "Thanks for this wonderful meal." Praying the meal means savoring the aroma, the color, the texture, the taste, remembering the Creator and those who produced and prepared it with conscious appreciation.

During your next meal, eat in silence for the first five minutes. Contemplate the food. What difference do you think this would make?

Have you ever eaten a meal in silence? I remember the first time I did, at a silent retreat. I could hardly stand it. The noise of the fork and knife hitting and scraping on metal plates. The sound of chewing—in stereo! I ate in five minutes and left.

But now I find it a joy. Eating the noon meal in silence with the monks at Saint Benedict's Monastery in Snowmass, Colorado, is a spiritual experience. I sit at the table looking out at snow-covered mountains and paying attention to each bite of lettuce, beans, curried stew, apple cake, each sip of wine or coffee. I receive these good gifts from the Giver of all good things. In the refectory I "taste and see that the Lord is good."

THE LORD'S SUPPER

That deep awareness of God's presence happens also in the chapel as we sing, pray, listen to Scripture, and especially as we eat and drink together in gratitude for and in remembrance of God's indescribable gift of Jesus Christ.

At the Last Supper, Jesus made his followers mindful of the ordinary as the symbol of real life. He took ordinary things of life, bread and wine, and gave them eternal significance. When Jesus broke the bread, gave thanks (mindful of where it came from), and shared it with his friends, he said, "This is my body, which is given for you. Do this in remembrance of me." A piece of bread full of life! Aah! And then he took a cup, gave thanks again (attentive to the One who gives life in abundance), and gave it to them, saying, "Drink from it, all of you, for this is my blood of the new covenant, which is poured out for many for the forgiveness of sins." A sip of wine bursting with meaning! Aah!

Is the celebration of Holy Communion a practice of awareness for you? Do you eat and drink mindfully?

Bread and wine were never the same again no matter how often they were eaten and drunk. They have become, for believers, a reminder of a deeper meaning of life, of a relationship with our Divine Friend, of the immediate Presence of God—as close to us as the food we digest.

It was so powerful a reminder that on Easter evening when Jesus broke bread in the home of two people in Emmaus, they recognized who he was. When he broke the bread, that dinner "table became a place of disclosure, recognition and revelation" (William Willimon, *Sunday Dinner,* p. 92). Their eyes were opened, and they saw! And they ran to the other disciples to tell them that Jesus was not gone but present.

And then Jesus appeared to all of them and said: "'Do you have anything to eat?' They gave him a piece of broiled fish, and he took it and ate in their presence." I imagine that for a long time eating fish made them attentive to Jesus' significance! The fish even became a logo for the early Christians. I have one on my front door to make myself and others aware that a friend of Jesus lives there.

Ever since those meals with Jesus, breaking bread has been important to Christians. The followers of Jesus ate together in remembrance of him. It was more than a way to recollect the memory of their famous friend. Remembrance really means *wake up, call to mind, reawaken!* It means paying attention! Jesus invites us to pay attention to him every time we eat a sandwich or drink a glass of wine. He invites us to remember that we are God's covenant people every time we receive a piece of bread or take a sip of wine during the Lord's Supper. We are to taste and see that the Lord is present and good! Paying attention and receptivity come together in a meal of grace.

THE LORD'S SUPPER AND THE LORD'S DAY

The Lord's Supper became a central event for the early Christians. They began meeting on Sunday evenings to commemorate the resurrection meal they had shared with Christ on Easter evening. Sunday became known as the Lord's Day, the day they celebrated the Lord's Supper. The shift from Saturday sabbath worship to Sunday celebration was gradual, and the details are lost in history. But some scholars think that the meeting of the risen Christ with his followers on Easter evening over a common meal greatly influenced the move to a Sunday observance (Paul Jewett, *The Lord's Day,* pp. 59-67). In remembrance of this important event, Christians gathered for table fellowship on the evening of the first day of the week.

When we observe sabbath time on Sunday and at Sunday worship, we are joining a practice with a long history in the church. It should be a time for fostering sabbath attitudes of rest, refreshment, receptivity, and attentiveness. A contemplative day of rest and worship.

Sabbath Time

Meditate on Paul's words "Persevere in prayer, with mind awake and thankful heart" (Col. 4:2). These can serve as a summary of this chapter. Or consider these words of this folk song written by Martin Bell:

> In a world full of mystery
> How I long to be like a newborn child.
> Seeing for the first time
> What was always there before my eyes. Now to
> my surprise—
> —© 1968, 1970 BY MARTIN BELL. *THE WAY OF THE WOLF*,
> BALLANTINE BOOKS, NEW YORK, NY.
> USED BY PERMISSION.

End with the familiar song "Open My Eyes" by Clara H. Scott.

Home Alone

Follow through on your pledge to pay attention during this week. By paying attention you will find inklings of God's grace during your day. By paying attention you will develop a sabbath attitude of receptivity.

Also read and meditate on chapter 5, "Sabbath as Release."

Make a pledge to God, yourself, and each other to be attentive this week, to develop a contemplative attitude that pays attention to nature, friends, family, fellow workers, and to God.

5

Sabbath
as Release

*For freedom Christ has set us free. Stand firm, therefore,
and do not submit again to a yoke of slavery.*

—GALATIANS 5:1

*The Lord is the Spirit, and where the Spirit of the Lord is,
there is freedom.*

—2 CORINTHIANS 3:17

Restful Beginning

Jesus invites us: "Come to me, you who are weary,
uptight, burdened, busy, and I will give you rest."

Take a few moments to do the following letting-go
exercise. If you are doing this with a group, have
someone lead you through the exercise. Pause for a
few moments between each of the following para-
graphs to do what is suggested.

Sit comfortably in your chair, hands on lap, palms up.
Think of things that hinder your relationship with
God:

- that keep you from praying
- that interfere with finding sabbath time
- that disturb times of silence
- that hamper your concentration as you come to
  this session

[pause]

Pile all your joys, sorrows, anxieties, concerns, plans,
pressures, and hopes in your hands like heaps of
sand.

[pause]

Now close your hands and clench your fists, as
though you are holding all those things tightly. Hang
on to them. Squeeze. Experience how tightly you
hold on.

[pause]

Hear Jesus' invitation to let go: "Come to me. . . . and I will give you rest."

Then gradually open your hands and let the concerns flow out through your fingers.

Relax and simply be in the presence of God. Be conscious of breathing in and out. Remember how God breathed into Adam's nostrils the breath of life and made him a living being. Remember how on that Easter evening, Jesus breathed on his disciples and said, "Receive the Holy Spirit."

Breathe in the life-giving Breath of God: "Receive the Holy Spirit." Then breathe out and say, "Into your hands I commit my spirit."

Be silent for a minute or more. End the silence by singing, "Breathe in the Spirit."

After ending, reflect on the letting-go meditation and on these words: "When you dare to let go and surrender [your] fears, your hand relaxes and your palms spread out in a gesture of receiving."

—HENRI NOUWEN

Reviewing

Review the past week. What was it like to pay close attention to nature, family, friends, fellow workers, and God? Discuss how that worked or did not work. Consider how such attentiveness could enhance your daily life.

Reflecting

FREEDOM FROM SLAVERY

As you respond to God's sabbath invitation to rest, refreshment, and receptivity, are you discovering that sabbath-keeping can be a *liberating* experience?

When I find a sabbath moment, hour, or day, it is like an island of calm in a hectic life. It is like a sigh of relief after putting down a knapsack full of obligations, schedules, and deadlines. It is like an invitation to enjoy a vacation with my Divine Friend. It feels like being unshackled from whatever I am allowing to enslave me and getting a new pespective on life.

That feeling is at the heart of sabbath-keeping. The fourth commandment calls for free time for people who had been enslaved: "Remember that you were a slave in the land of Egypt, and the LORD your God brought you out from there with a mighty hand and an outstretched arm; *therefore* the LORD your God commanded you to keep the sabbath day" (Deut. 5:15).

> *The Deuteronomy reason for Sabbath-keeping is that our ancestors in Egypt went for four hundred years without a vacation (Deut. 5:15). Never a day off. The consequence: they were no longer considered persons but slaves. Hands. Work units. Not persons created in the image of God but equipment for making brick and building pyramids. Humanity was defaced.*
> —EUGENE PETERSON, WORKING THE ANGLES, P. 49

Slaves lose their dignity and identity. Are there situations when you feel enslaved, merely a work unit?

God's enormous act of grace ("I am the LORD your God who brought you out . . .") was followed by an invitation to live into that freedom: "You shall have no other gods besides me" (Ex. 20:2-3). It sounds like a restriction, but it is actually a relief. The only God is the One who liberates us!

This God gave ten great freedoms to shape the lives of the liberated. One of them provided for free time once a week to remember the Savior and savor our release from oppression and slavery. It is striking that this time off was not limited to rabbis, or monks, or employers, or to the rich. It was also for daughters, sons, workers, slaves, guests, strangers, even animals. Everyone was to stop work! No social or spiritual elitism. On the sabbath everyone was to stop, rest, and catch their breath.

Sabbath as rest for everyone is a revolutionary idea. It is a powerful social statement with ethical implications. It implies that "God is linked to the human needs of the lowest bonded servant. Both Yahweh and the exhausted slave need to stop and catch their breath, to look up from the task at hand. As the sovereign of the universe, Yahweh can presumably pause whenever he chooses. But the kitchen slave and the grape picker must be protected by divine law from the greed and insensitivity of the rich" (Harvey Cox, *Turning East*, pp. 68-69).

This commandment is as much for the enslavers as for the enslaved, for employers as for employees, for professors as for students. It seems so difficult for those in power—the bosses, the professors, the elite—to allow those not in power a time of refreshment, relaxation, rest, and refocusing. So "the sabbath discipline is not just an option. It is a legal mandate in order to insure the extension of its full benefits to the poor and the powerless" (p. 69).

The Exodus 31 version of the sabbath rule underlines its seriousness by imposing the death penalty on anyone who works or who makes someone else work on the sabbath. A bit heavy! But a strong reminder that such a time for rest and appreciation of freedom from slavery is a basic human right. (See Tilden Edwards, *Sabbath Time*, pp. 86-92.)

ACCEPTED BY GRACE

Sabbath affirms the dignity of all people. When no one is working, it is hard to tell the difference between them by their achievements. They are equal as imagebearers of God, as persons loved by God! So sabbath is a sign of divine grace, a reminder of who we are before God. We have value beyond what we produce or achieve. In fact, we are accepted by God before we do or achieve anything important. Our identity and dignity are given by the God who created and redeemed us. We do not work to merit salvation. It is given to us.

In John Calvin's view, the sabbath calls the faithful to "refrain from their own works, in order to leave God to work within them." We not only rest from our daily work, but "abandon completely our own works as a basis for our relationship with God, for that relationship is grounded in grace" (John Primus, *Calvin and the Puritan Sabbath*, p. 60). In fact, "God's will for us in the fourth commandment" is that, not only on the sabbath day, but "every day of my life I rest from my

> Heschel says the Sabbath is a day "in which we are what we are, regardless of whether we are learned or not, of whether our career is a success or a failure; it is a day of independence of social conditions." Do you experience this in your Sunday gatherings?

evil ways, let the Lord work in me through his Spirit, and so begin already in this life the eternal Sabbath" (Heidelberg Catechism, Q & A 103). For Christians, "the sabbath expresses the heart of the Good News that God in Christ reveals an infinite love for us that does not depend on our works" (Tilden Edwards, p. 91). It is not only free time, but freedom time. A holy day of freedom.

As Lord of the sabbath, Jesus affirmed this liberating understanding. When he healed "a woman with a spirit that had crippled her for eighteen years," he was criticized for doing this on the sabbath. His provocative answer: "And ought not this woman, a daughter of Abraham whom Satan bound for eighteen long years, be set free from this bondage on the sabbath day?" (Luke 13:16).

FRIENDS OF GOD

Paul declares freedom time also for Christians. "For freedom Christ has set us free. . . . do not submit again to a yoke of slavery" (Gal. 5:1). One of the last things Jesus says to his followers is, "I do not call you servants any longer" (John 15:15). How about that for a radical invitation to freedom! What a relief for duty-prone Christians! Jesus calls us friends.

How do you respond to Jesus' words "I have called you friends"? Does that seem appropriate? Fitting? Appealing?

What an invitation to an intimate and mature relationship! In servanthood there is neither maturity nor intimacy. Someone else runs the show, makes the decisions, carries out the responsibilities. A servant follows orders, without personal dignity or full personal worth.

The good news is that we can live as friends of Christ, with all the intimacy, maturity, risk, confidence, strength, and joy that implies. To experience friendship with God is to celebrate our freedom in Christ—freedom from fear into strength, freedom from cowering into confidence that our insights, likes, dislikes, ideas, and experiences are valued. We can experience unconditional acceptance by God.

What is your own particular way of being a friend with God? How do you maintain that friendship?

Friendship with God is one biblical image I find very helpful in developing a sabbath attitude. It's an image that gives us enormous dignity and invites us to an adult and mature relationship with God. Each of us brings our own personality, gifts, idiosyncrasies, and strengths to our friendship with God. We don't have to imitate someone else's relationship with God. We can be ourselves with God. How comforting! How freeing!

When the invitation to a sabbath vacation comes from our divine Friend, it is compelling. Taking time with a friend is less a duty than a privilege. We don't have to be commanded to spend time with a friend. It's a joy to be together. We know the relationship will die if we don't stay in touch.

How do friends stay in touch? They make five-minute phone calls, take half-hour walks, talk over dinner, and share intimate silences. They write notes and letters. They go on trips together. They argue, weather estrangement and hostility, put up with each other's idiosyncrasies, risk being vulnerable. Friends have conflicts and reconciliations. Friends even serve each other (John 15:13). But their serving arises out of love and compassion and caring, not out of duty and servitude. And that makes all the difference.

Friends want to be together as often as possible. Experiencing God as our Friend can make us seek sabbath time more often. We may find out that the sabbath was made just for us, and not we for the sabbath (as Jesus taught in Mark 2:27). Developing a sabbath discipline based on staying in touch with our Friend is more a joy than drudgery. Frequent conversations can make God's presence and power more real to us. Realizing that our Friend is present right now, right here, can make us relish the sacredness of each moment.

PRAISE AND PLAY

Freedom with our Friend releases us for celebration and play. Sabbath-keeping can become sabbath-living and even sabbath-playing! The sabbath is not only for contemplation but also for celebration. It is for festival, for feasting, rejoicing, and praise. Psalm 92 is "A Song for the Sabbath Day":

> *It is good to praise you, Lord,*
> *and to sing to your name, O God on high,*
> *proclaiming each morning that you are faithful,*
> *each evening that we can trust you,*
> *using ten-stringed lyre and harp,*
> *using sounds of music.*
> *Lord, you have made me delight in your actions;*
> *I celebrate what your hands have done.*
> *How great are your deeds, O Lord!*
>
> —VV. 1-5, *THE PSALMS, A NEW TRANSLATION FOR PRAYER AND WORSHIP,* TRANSLATED BY GARY CHAMBERLAIN. © 1984, THE UPPER ROOM. USED BY PERMISSION.

According to the Heidelberg Catechism, sabbath is meant to be "a festive day of rest." Do you experience it as such a joyful time? What could you do to make it more of a festival?

When I was in Israel, I celebrated three sabbaths with Jewish families. Each one was a celebrative occasion. The whole family gathered together. The house was made ready. Special foods were prepared. Prayers were offered to welcome in the Queen of Sabbath in joy and peace, like a radiant bride. While the sabbath candles were lit, prayers were offered for enlightening the home and heart of the family with love, joy, and happiness. For these families, sabbath was the happiest day of the week.

Those at The Desert House of Prayer just outside Tucson, Arizona, also know how to celebrate Sunday joyously. Each day of the week begins with silent meditation from 5:15 to 6:15 a.m. Then comes Mass, then silence for the whole day until dinner. But on Sunday it is different. Evening Mass is held early, so everyone can have a festive dinner together. Wine is served before and during dinner. The table is specially decorated and a fine meal is served, establishing a jovial mood.

And then after the dishes are done, we all gather for a *listening hour*—sitting in the library/living room and listening for an hour to recorded classical music. No reading. No conversation. No writing. Just receiving the music. This is my ideal for every Sunday evening. Closing Sunday/sabbath observance with a party!

Sabbath is meant for joy. Paul's words in Philippians 4:4, "Rejoice in the Lord always; again I will say, Rejoice," serve as a good sabbath motto. Once again, it is the grace of God that gives us this joyful perspective on the world. When we observe sabbath on Sunday to commemorate the first day of creation and the day of Jesus' resurrection and the coming of the Holy Spirit, we are celebrating the highlights of God's gracious activity.

Is the sabbath a day of prayer for you? Can you also make it a day of play? Think of ways you could play on this holy day.

Such grace gives comic relief in an over-serious world. It gives us back our sense of wonder and awe. It gives dreams to those who are jaded. It gives play in a gloomy world. It gives the sabbath in a world bound to work or frenzied leisure. "The Sabbath is a sign that God has written over man: 'Destined for Playfulness.' ... Play ... is a parable to illuminate the reality of a free grace that transforms a bitterly serious life into a life of playful hope" (Lewis Smedes, *God and the Good,* pp. 59-60). I like to call the sabbath the Playday of Grace. It is a day and a time not only to breathe in the Spirit, but to dance with the Spirit in the joy of freedom (see Ps. 150).

In his article "Confessions of a Former Sabbath-Breaker," Eugene Peterson urges us to consider the sabbath as a time to play as well as to pray. In worship, he says, we exercise our bodies and minds and spirits in acts of adoration and commitment, supplication and praise, forgiving and giving. But to be complete, we also play (*Christianity Today,* Sept. 2, 1988, pp. 25-28).

In play, we exercise our bodies, minds, and spirit in games and walks, in amusement and reading, in visiting and picnicking, in puttering and writing. We let the creativity of the creation nudge us into creativity.

We surprise ourselves by creating a meal, a conversation, or some laughter. We have some fun.

For Peterson, good sabbath-keeping includes both praying and playing. Prayerful sabbaths without play or playful sabbaths without prayer are only half-sabbaths. Prayer without play can degenerate into a dutiful but cheerless religion. Play without prayer can become mind-numbing escape.

So when you are looking for ways to catch your breath, think of ways to play. Protect the leisure for praying and playing! Sabbath as a playday and prayerday of grace can give friends of God joy and freedom to take along into the whole week and into eternity.

Sabbath Time

As a way to close your session, take five minutes to listen to a reading of Psalm 92:1-5 or Psalm 150. Meditate on them as ways to celebrate sabbath time. Then finish with a prayer or song of praise (perhaps "What a Friend We Have in Jesus").

Home Alone

Read John 15:12-17, particularly verse 15: "I do not call you servants any longer.... I have called you friends." Hear those words as a personal invitation. Contemplate that invitation for a few minutes.

Then write down some of the qualities or characteristics you value in a friend. What does *friend* mean to you? Write as many words as you can think of that describe what you look for in friendship.

Follow that by sitting in a meditative posture and attitude and going over your list slowly. Savor each word as a description of God's friendship with you. Take your time. Prayerfully reflect on how knowing God as a Friend would change, enhance, deepen your relationship. You might also write a prayer to God as your Friend.

Close by singing or saying the hymn "What a Friend We Have in Jesus."

During the week, read and reflect thoughtfully on chapter 6, "Sabbath as Refocusing."

6

Sabbath
as Refocusing

Draw near to God, and he will draw near to you.

—JAMES 4:8

For me it is good to be near God.

—PSALM 73:28

Restful Beginning

Begin a time of quiet reflection by reading and meditating on these words from Psalm 73:

I look to no one else in heaven,
I delight in nothing else on earth.
My flesh and my heart are pining with love,
my heart's Rock, my own, God for ever!
My joy lies in being close to God.
I have taken shelter in the Lord,
continually to proclaim what you have done.

—VV. 25-26, 28, JERUSALEM BIBLE

After a few minutes with the text, let these words of Abraham Kuyper deepen your understanding and experience of being near to God:

To be "near" is to be so close to God that your eye sees, your heart is aware of, and your ear hears him, and every cause of separation has been removed. . . . This knowledge of God comes . . . when the Lord has become a Personal Presence by the side of your own self; when God and you have entered into a conscious, vital, personal, particular relationship . . . the most intimate fellowship conceivable in heaven and on earth—He your Father, your shepherd, your bosom Friend and your God!

[A] meeting takes place—a moment of such blessedness as can never be expressed in words. . . . A mystical, most intimate and personal love in [your] own heart . . . blessedness that exceeds everything that can be imagined. Then it is good, Oh! so good—above all things else—to be near to your God.

—TO BE NEAR UNTO GOD, PP. 22-23

After reflecting for a few minutes on these words, end by singing "Breathe in the Spirit" and praying.

Reviewing

After your time of meditation discuss your experience. Are there times that you are near to God? When are these? What occasions them?

Discuss your meditations on "God as Friend" during the past week and your experiences of staying in touch with your Divine Friend. Did you feel close to your Divine Friend?

Reflecting

BACK IN FOCUS

When I wake up in the morning and look around, the world looks like a Renoir painting, everything a little blurred and out of focus. Then I fumble around, find my trifocals, put them on, and my world is back in focus. I can see more clearly what I'm doing and where I'm going.

Sunday sabbath time does that for my inner sight. The ringing of the bell of my childhood church invited me to wake up and to focus on God through the spectacles of a sabbath attitude. The bell is gone, but I still need the spectacles!

Do you need, again and again, to refocus your vision, your priorities, your life? How do you accomplish that?

Not that I completely forget about God during the week. But often the vision of God's presence gets blurred; my priorities get jumbled; my commitments seem unclear. My perspective narrows to the mundane. I'm often influenced by a *this-is-all-there-is-there-ain't-no-more* secularism: sabbath helps me celebrate a *there's-more-than-meets-the-eye* reality. It urges me to lift my gaze from the mundane to the lofty.

It's something like what happened to an art student friend. Sue looked mostly at the ground, painting what she saw around her. One day she looked up and noticed how much there was in the sky; how much she had been missing by always looking down. Her looking up was spiritual as well as physical. She began painting what she saw in the sky—the wondrous colors and shapes. Her large painting of abstract swishes of red, yellow, orange, and blue in my office is her response to the dawning of an Easter morning and to the resurrection of Christ in her heart. Sue's upward gaze not only refocused her artistic perspective but also refocused her life on the holy, on God. She realized *there's-more-than-meets-the-eye!*

Sabbath provides us artists-of-life an opportunity for that radical kind of refocusing. It is a chance to lift our gaze to the sacred, to readjust our minds, realign our hearts, reset our priorities, clarify our commitments, and enlarge our perspective. We realize that there is another reality beyond the ordinary, eager to break through. Sabbath is like a guest waiting to be welcomed. It is a promise that we can be near to God, since God comes near to us (James 4:8). The Holy in our midst; or is it that we are in the midst of the Holy?

FOCUS ON THE HOLY

The sabbath invites us to become attuned to "holiness in time" (Heschel, *The Sabbath,* p. 10). "Remember the sabbath day to keep it *holy"* is an opportunity to sense the sacred, to open ourselves to the reality of the holy, to realize there is more than meets the eye. Much more. Sabbath is a time for being in the presence of the holy and letting the holy shape our lives (Reformed theologians call this sanctification). An awesome, sanctifying possibility.

What is that awareness of the holy like? I imagine it is different for different people. I remember being in Denali National Park in Alaska. I and my eleven-year-old granddaughter were looking at the tallest mountain in the United States, Mount McKinley. I asked her how she felt. She replied with the profound simplicity of a child, "Kinda little!" She was in awe. Does that come close to the feeling?

I was walking on the Continental Divide in Costa Rica with my wife, Elaine. All of a sudden we came

> Discuss this quote: "The creature's proper mode of speech about creation is not description but lyric, not argumentation but poetry . . . [and] extended doxology."
> —WALTER BRUEGGEMANN

upon an opening in the trees and a breathtaking vista stretching out for miles. We stood there with tears streaming down our faces, hardly knowing why.

We had a similar experience one Sunday afternoon in a museum called "The Biblical Message of Marc Chagall" in Nice, France. We were moved to tears again as we encountered the sacred in Chagall's paintings of stories from Genesis and Exodus. There's more than meets the eye! We were moved to doxology and worship in an unlikely place.

It can happen anywhere. If God is present anywhere, at any time, it is right here, right now. It occurred to me in the middle of downtown Chicago with cars honking, taxis weaving in and out, trains clanging overhead, harried people rushing every which way—noise, clamor, busyness. I was heartened that I could sense the nearness of God also in the frenzy of the city, since we live our lives there more often than in quiet places in nature or on retreat.

Sacred moments happen to people at a concert, at the birth of a child, when they face grave illness, and when they go through death with a loved one. My daughter-in-law's mother died within five weeks of finding out she had lung cancer. During those five weeks family and friends visited, expressed gratitude, grieved, and said goodbye. She embodied one of her favorite quotes: "To be a witness means we live in such a way that our lives would not make sense if God did not exist." Somehow we all sensed the presence of God with her and through her. We experienced God as a source of strength and courage and the secret of inner freedom. Her death brought her—and us—face to face with God.

Recall a personal experience of the holy, the sacred, a time when you felt near to God.

Encounters with the holy can happen anywhere and can move us to wonder and worship. We need such experiences from nature or Scripture to help us retain the memory in our soul of the high, the holy, and the eternal. Sabbath gives us an opportunity to refocus on the holy presence of God, to "give thanks to the LORD with [our] whole heart . . . [for] holy and awesome is his name" (Ps. 111:1, 9).

FOCUS ON WORSHIP

Read aloud Isaiah 6:1-8 for yet another experience of the holy. Reflect on the prophet's experience of wonder, confession, worship, and surrender.

The holy evokes worship. Sabbath is first of all about work and rest. But it also is about worship and rejoicing, a time to "worship the Lord in the beauty of holiness" (Ps. 29:2). Sabbath worship provides time and space to be near to God, for, through his Word and Spirit, God is powerfully present with us. Worship gives Christians the opportunity to stay in touch with the risen Christ. Sunday has become the day for many Christians to heed the invitation to sabbath rest and the invitation to sabbath worship.

It wasn't always like that. In the beginning of the Christian movement, Sunday was not a day off. It was not a sabbath time of rest. It was just another work day. Jewish Christians in Jerusalem and Israel attended synagogue on Saturday for worship just as Jesus had done. That was their day off, their sabbath.

But there was also something about the first day of the week that compelled them to gather as a community. Even though they didn't have Sunday off, Jewish and Gentile Christians would gather after work on the first day of the week. Justin Martyr (d. A.D. 165) tells us they gathered for baptism, reading of Scripture, teaching, prayer, and as a culmination, the breaking of the bread—the remembrance of their risen Lord.

As the day for the Christian sabbath gradually shifted from Saturday to Sunday, Christians continued to get together weekly. There was something divinely inspired about a weekly day set apart to focus on God. The rhythm now, however, is not six days and then one, but one day and then six. Beginning the week with a celebration of the resurrection gives the week a focus. It celebrates God's grace as the basis for all that happens in our lives. Sunday/sabbath time refocuses our lives on worship.

How do you prepare for worship? Do you take the time to refocus before coming into the presence of your Divine Friend?

Christians' gathering on Sunday celebrates the Easter event. It also celebrates Pentecost and the Spirit of freedom who inspires us.

Worship is not first of all entertainment or evangelism or even instruction. We do not worship to get something. The primary focus of meaningful worship is God, God's presence and grace. Worship opens with God's gracious greeting and offer of acceptance, pardon, and forgiveness. We realize that we are on holy ground. Isaiah's experience (6:1-8) provides a model for our worship.

If we aren't prepared for this, we can miss it. Tilden Edwards urges us to surround our Sunday worship with sabbath attitudes and gives helpful suggestions about both our preparations and celebrations:

> *Corporate worship, in order to be its intended self, needs to be surrounded by a protective time zone, a time of preparation and reflection, of quiet openness with nothing to do except appreciate the presence of God in the smallest random thing in and around us. If this is done, then corporate worship is more likely to become a radiant crystal whose facets catch up all of life in God's light, placed in the midst of a velvet sabbath bed that sets it off. Without such surrounding sabbath time, worship more likely will resemble an opaque rock which reveals nothing of life's giftedness and integrity in God, only our own rushed anxiety.*
> —SABBATH TIME, PP. 78-79

Worship can provide a chance to rest and be attentive to the divine dimensions of life. It can provide time and space to simply breathe in the holy Breath of God. Some silence in the torrent of words and music. Two minutes of silence at various times in the worship can be a beginning. At a meditative service I have experienced ten minutes or more of silence as an awesome time of refreshment and receptivity.

Worship also challenges us to allow the reverence we experience in God's presence—as we pray, hear God's Word, celebrate the sacraments—to shape our lives, to carry the new life we celebrate into the ordinary life of our week, and to realign our lives with God's priorities.

Do works of compassion flow out of your sabbaths?

FOCUS ON COMPASSION

Compassion is one of God's priorities. We didn't do much on Sundays in my childhood, but we did go out on Sunday afternoons to sing for people in nursing homes. We would talk with the people and give them a tract. (I remember one Sunday we had tracts on marrying the right partner. It seemed a bit out of place. But the people appreciated our visit anyway.) Sometimes we went to downtown Chicago to sing at the Helping Hand Mission on skid row (as it was called), or to the poor house, or a jail. This was a day for showing mercy and doing good deeds.

Compassion is a focus that Jesus gave to the sabbath. As a devout Jew, he certainly kept the sabbath, yet he had a very open attitude toward the traditions of sabbath-keeping. He was criticized for healing, on the sabbath, a man with a withered right hand and a woman who had been crippled for eighteen years (Luke 6:6-11; 13:10-17). By these actions, Jesus showed his freedom in relation to the sabbath and his understanding of the sabbath as a day meant for the good of human beings (Mark 2:27). "Keeping the sabbath day holy" obviously includes compassion.

> *Because God's eternity enfolds us in our Sabbath celebrations . . . we will delight in becoming agents for [God's] purpose of caring for the poor, delivering the oppressed, announcing the good news of salvation, building peace in the world—not with any false idealism that we can bring the kingdom of God to its culmination in the world, but with the sure hope that God is always at work to create peace and justice and freedom and that we can participate in his eternal purpose because of the Holy Spirit's power within and through us.*
> —MARVA DAWN, *KEEPING THE SABBATH WHOLLY,* PP. 164-5

Nearness to God, experienced at sabbath moments and celebrated in worship, can permeate and give color to our feeling, perceptions, thinking, imagining, willing, acting, speaking. It can be a passion that

Sabbath is an intuition of eternity. Reflect on this quote: "Unless one learns how to relish the taste of Sabbath while still in this world, unless one is initiated in the appreciation of eternal life, one will be unable to enjoy the taste of eternity in the world to come."

—ABRAHAM
JOSHUA HESCHEL

breathes through our whole existence now and into eternity.

FOCUS ON ETERNAL SABBATH

Besides worship and compassion, John Calvin suggested a third purpose for keeping the sabbath: to meditate upon the final sabbath rest at the end of life. This is also reflected in the Heidelberg Catechism: "God's will for [me] in the fourth commandment [is] that every day of my life I rest from my evil ways, let the Lord work in me through his Spirit, and so begin already in this life the eternal Sabbath" (Q & A 103). Sabbath involves an openness to surprise in the future! The thrust of the sabbath is into eternity.

The writer to the Hebrews brings our exploration full circle, connecting the Genesis 2 statement about God's resting on the seventh day with our final salvation as rest in God's presence. "A sabbath rest still remains for the people of God; for those who enter God's rest also cease from their labors as God did from his. Let us therefore make every effort to enter that rest" (4:9-11).

We are practicing the scales of sabbath now so that we can play in the sabbath orchestra in eternity. The restful stream of Psalm 23 becomes "the river of the water of life, bright as crystal, flowing from the throne of God and of the Lamb through the middle of the street of the city" (Rev. 22:1-2). In that eternal sabbath, we will join with people from every nation in singing, "Holy, Holy, Holy."

The psalmist says, "O God . . . my soul thirsts for you" (Ps. 63:1). Have you experienced that thirsting for God?

CONCLUSION

When we get into sabbath time, the horizon never seems to end, does it? As we have explored various aspects of the sabbath, I have felt like we were trying to catch Niagara Falls in a cup! It seems impossible to contain it all. We have caught just a trickle of the vast meaning of this enormous gift. Yet I, for one, have caught enough to make me thirsty for more. How about you?

I have realized that I don't need to grasp everything about sabbath or put into practice everything I've learned to make it meaningful. Rather than working hard at keeping sabbath, perhaps I can surrender to the sabbath attitudes that can keep me. I seem to be in a gradual process of accepting God's gracious invitation to sabbath rest. And I want to continue in that process. Will you join me?

Consider which of all the attitudes and practices we have explored you would like to continue. For, as I said at the beginning, the benefit of sabbath is not only in thinking about it but in doing it, in living the sabbath, in being a sabbath person.

Consider what ideas and attitudes have become important for your spiritual formation, what sabbath practices will keep you focused on God and help you stay in touch with your Divine Friend. What will you do—or not do—to make sabbath part of the rhythm of your life? What will help you catch your breath often so you can breathe the Breath of God now and into the eternal sabbath? These attitudes and practices are the cup we use to catch for ourselves a little of the vast meaning of sabbath and of the God of the sabbath.

May the Holy One whose name is Surprise fill you with unexpected peace, joy, and hope as you live into the divine rhythm of this holy time!

Sabbath Time

You may wish to plan a bit more time for closing this session. Spend it first of all discussing what concepts and attitudes in this study have been particularly meaningful for you, and what practices were helpful in fostering sabbath living for you.

Then write some specific sabbath practices you want to develop over the next month. Choose practices that will provide rest, refreshment, receptivity, freedom, and focus for you. What will be sabbath reminders for you?

Close with "Breathe in the Spirit," the theme song of this book, which focuses us on the spirit of compassion in sabbath living. Add a prayer for courage and persistence to carry out the sabbath practices you have promised yourself and God.

Home Alone

For the next month, continue whatever sabbath practices you have established. Then take a look at how you've been doing. Revise your practice in a way that makes it more realistic. You may wish to cut back a little or to challenge yourself a little more. You will probably continue to revise your practice, subtracting or adding to it, as you grow in your spiritual life.

Some time during this next week you might also read and reflect on the epilogue in this book, either personally or as a group. You may find it helpful also to join with others who will keep you accountable for the path you have chosen. It is much easier when you are doing this with someone else. That's something of what the Christian community, the church, is all about!

Epilogue

A Personal
Experience

I leave you with one meaningful experience of sabbath as a stimulus to further reflection and discussion.

On my journey toward a deeper understanding and celebration of the sabbath, I remind myself of a weekend I spent at Saint Benedict's Monastery, Snowmass, Colorado. The monastery is located in a valley surrounded on all four sides by mountains.

I awakened early on Sunday morning so that I could attend Vigils—early morning prayers—at 2:55 a.m. The monastery bell called us to prayer. The first words that were spoken in the chapel were, "O Lord, open my lips that my mouth may show forth your praise." Fitting first words for the beginning of the day. There were psalms, prayers, silence.

At 3:45 a.m. I went outside and watched the stars. I then joined the monks from 4:00-4:30 a.m. for a half hour of silent meditation. I went back to my room for tea, some reading, and to watch the day unfold.

In the pitch-black of night I could barely see the mountains. Then, as the light gradually appeared around 5:00 a.m., the mountains emerged. The tip of snow-covered Mount Sopris appeared out of the darkness like magic. The trees showed up on the mountains. Then the valley. Nothing was rushed. It was accompanied by the singing of the birds—a slow, peaceful way to begin the day. Different from jumping out of bed as the alarm clock rudely calls my soul back and jars me awake.

Back in the chapel for solemn worship and Eucharist, a little conversation, and a meal in meditative silence. Then a whole day with nowhere to go and nothing to do. I had no car to escape the solitude and no way out of the valley. I lay in the grass, watched clouds, admired the hills. I walked for a few hours, embraced by beauty. I read a bit, wrote, prayed, napped, and reflected on life.

An *aah* experience of wordless admiration and praise and gratitude. Receiving gifts of God. Rest and refreshment. Freedom. Opening my mind and heart so God could fill them.

Evening prayers ended the day with the prayer, "Into your hands, O Lord, I commit my spirit."

A tryst with God. A time to catch a whiff of God's grace. A sabbath experience like that cannot be rushed. It needs some leisure. When my life seems like a runaway semi plunging down a Colorado mountain highway without a driver, such a sabbath time is like a runaway-truck runway that slows me and keeps me from disaster!

Since I have had that experience, I have been able to recapture it at various times. On a Sunday morning during worship. Sometimes as I sit in my backyard, or walk in the woods or around the neighborhood. Even sitting behind my desk and spending five minutes in contemplation, or in just breathing—breathing the pure breath and vitality of God's Spirit. I long for more experiences like that. In fact, as I am recalling this experience, I realize how much I need to take a break from activity to catch my breath, receive the grace of God, and savor the sacredness of the moment—for my spiritual health. How about you?

If you refrain from trampling the sabbath,
from pursuing your own interests on my holy day;
if you call the sabbath a delight
and the holy day of the Lord honorable;
if you honor it, not going your own ways,
serving your own interests, or pursuing your own affairs;
then you shall take delight in the LORD,
and I will make you ride upon the heights of the earth.
—ISAIAH 58:13-14

Breathe in the Spirit

Slowly

Stephen Rush

Breathe in the Spir - rit Breathe out com-pass - ion.

C Maj.7   D   G   C   a minor   D   G   C

Breathe in the Spir - rit Breathe out com-pass - ion.

Appendix A

SOURCES AND AUTHORS
OF MARGIN QUOTATIONS

CHAPTER 1

Abraham Joshua Heschel. *The Sabbath: Its Meaning for Modern Man*. New York: Farrar, Straus & Giroux, 1951, p. 29.

Heschel, 18.

Heschel, 8.

Heschel, 10.

Heschel, 29.

CHAPTER 2

Heschel, 14.

Heschel, 14.

Heschel, 32.

Matthew Kelty. *Flute Solo, Reflections of a Trappist Monk*. Garden City, NY: Doubleday & Co., Image Books, 1980, p. 14.

CHAPTER 3

Thomas Merton. *Thoughts in Solitude*. New York: Farrar, Straus & Giroux, 1956, p. 42.

Heschel, 83.

Heschel, 29.

CHAPTER 4

Heschel, 22-23.

CHAPTER 5

Henri J. M. Nouwen. *With Open Hands*. Notre Dame, Ind.: Ave Maria Press, 1972, p. 17.

Heschel, 30.

CHAPTER 6

Walter Brueggemann. *Interpretation: A Bible Commentary for Teaching and Preaching: Genesis*. Atlanta: John Knox Press, 1982, p. 27-28.

Heschel, 74.

Bibliography

Barry, William A. and William J. Connolly. *The Practice of Spiritual Direction*. New York: The Seabury Press, Inc., 1982.

Battles, Ford Lewis. *The Piety of John Calvin*. Grand Rapids, Mich.: Baker Book House, 1978.

Bell, Martin. *The Way of the Wolf: The Gospel in New Images*. New York: The Seabury Press, Inc., 1970.

Berry, Wendell. *Sabbaths*. San Francisco: North Point Press, 1987.

Brueggemann, Walter. *Interpretation: A Bible Commentary for Teaching and Preaching: Genesis*. Atlanta: John Knox Press, 1982.

Callahan, William R. *Noisy Contemplation*. Quixote Center, P.O. Box 5206, Hyattsville, MD 20782, 1982. (This is an amazing book that encourages prayer for ordinary people in the middle of living their lives. It is printed as a tabloid newspaper so people and groups can afford it.)

Calvin, John. *Institutes of the Christian Religion*. Translated by John Allen, Grand Rapids, Mich.: Wm. B. Eerdmans Publishing Co., 1949.

Canham, Elizabeth J. "A Rest Remaining," *Weavings*, March/April 1993. Published by The Upper Room, Nashville, Tenn.

Cox, Harvey. *Turning East*. New York: A Touchstone Book by Simon and Schuster, 1977. (I am indebted to Cox for pointing out *catch your breath* as a possible interpretation of rest, and thus for the title of this book.)

Dawn, Marva J. *Keeping the Sabbath Wholly: Ceasing, Resting, Embracing, Feasting*. Grand Rapids, Mich.: Wm. B. Eerdmans Publishing Co., 1989.

Eck, Diana L. *Encountering God*. Boston: Beacon Press, 1993.

Edwards, Tilden. *Sabbath Time*. Nashville, Tenn.: Upper Room Books, 1992.

Hanh, Thich Nhat. *Peace Is Every Step: The Path of Mindfulness in Everyday Life*. New York: Bantam Books, 1992.

Heschel, Abraham Joshua. *The Sabbath*. New York: Farrar, Straus & Giroux, Inc., 1951, 1979. (seventeenth printing, 1990)

Jewett, Paul K. *The Lord's Day: A Theological Guide to the Christian Day of Worship*. Grand Rapids, Mich.: Wm. B. Eerdmans Publishing Co., 1971.

Kelty, Matthew. *Flute Solo: Reflections of a Trappist Hermit.* Garden City, N.Y.: Doubleday & Co., Inc., Image Books, 1980.

Kushner, Lawrence. *GOD was in this PLACE & I, i did not know.* Woodstock, Vt.: Jewish Lights Publishing, 1991.

Kuyper, Abraham. *Near Unto God.* Adapted for Contemporary Christians by James Calvin Schaap. Grand Rapids, Mich.: co-published by CRC Publications and Wm. B. Eerdmans Publishing Co., 1997.

Kuyper, Abraham. *To Be Near Unto God.* Grand Rapids, Mich.: Baker Book House, 1925.

Loder, Ted. *Guerrillas of Grace: Prayers for the Battle.* San Diego: LuraMedia, 1984.

Merton, Thomas. *Thoughts in Solitude.* New York: Farrar, Straus & Giroux, 1956, 1958. Renewed in 1986.

Nouwen, Henri J. M. *With Open Hands.* Notre Dame, Ind.: Ave Maria Press, 1972.

Palmer, Parker J. *The Active Life: A Spirituality of Work, Creativity, and Caring.* San Francisco: Harper & Row, Publishers, Inc., 1990.

Peterson, Eugene. "Confessions of a Former Sabbath-Breaker," *Christianity Today,* Sept. 2, 1988, pp. 25-28.

_____. *Working the Angles.* Grand Rapids, Mich.: Wm. B. Eerdmans Publishing Co., 1987.

_____. *The Message: The New Testament in Contemporary English.* Colorado Springs: Navpress, 1993.

Primus, John H. "Calvin and the Puritan Sabbath: A Comparative Study," *Exploring the Heritage of John Calvin,* ed. David Holwerda. Grand Rapids, Mich.: Baker Book House, 1976.

Rice, Howard. *Reformed Spirituality: An Introduction for Believers.* Louisville, Ky.: Westminister/John Knox Press, 1991.

Rupp, Joyce. "Instruments of God," *May I Have This Dance?* Notre Dame, Ind.: Ave Maria Press, 1992.

Smedes, Lewis. "Theology and the Playful Life," *God and the Good.* Grand Rapids, Mich.: Wm. B. Eerdmans Publishing Co., 1975.

Smith, Martin L. *A Season for the Spirit.* Cambridge: Cowley Publications, 1991. (This is one of the best books I have ever used for Lenten study and spiritual reading. I also found the image of catching Niagara Falls in a cup from him.)

The Psalms: A New Translation for Prayer and Worship. Transl. Gary Chamberlain. Nashville, Tenn: The Upper Room, 1984.

Willimon, William H. *Sunday Dinner: The Lord's Supper and the Christian Life.* Nashville, Tenn.: The Upper Room, 1981.